Stephen K. De Silva

PROSPEROUS SOUL

REVISED EDITION

FOUNDATIONS

THE COMPANION COURSE TO
Money and the Prosperous Soul

Prosperous Soul: Foundations
© Copyright 2018 Stephen K. De Silva
Written by Stephen K. De Silva
Published by De Silva Ministries
Book Cover Design by Joshua Read
Book Formatting: Simeon Chard
Printed in the United States of America

ISBN: 978-0-9968853-8-6

ACKNOWLEDGES

Cory, Colleen, Timothy, and Autumn: For you, I would fight a bear—and win

TABLE OF CONTENTS.

PREFACE

Welcome to the revised *Prosperous Soul Foundations Course*. This edition is much more cohesive and well laid out than the original. The earliest version of this manual was first released in 2005, while I was still developing the Prosperous Soul material in my classes at Bethel Church. It worked well as an in-depth study for my students and the many others who picked it up, but as time passed, I realized some changes needed to be made.

The original manual was bulky in its format and clunky in its delivery. By shortening, moving, and removing some of the technical components, I was able to create a more consistent and connected course. I then turned my attention to cleaning up the design and removing some of the distracting components. I am convinced these changes make *Prosperous Soul: Foundations* more manageable and easier to read.

In my efforts to improve this manual, I also looked at the complementary components of this curriculum. In the accompanying videos, I reedited the content into bite-sized digital files so that the visual content better matches the written material, allowing the readers to learn more effectively. As I edited down the manual for the individual reader, I pulled out the technical information and added some tools and strategies to create a brand new leader's guide.

I am happy to have you on this journey and I pray the Lord leads you into incredible breakthrough. If you wish to go deeper than the *Foundations Course*, consider looking into my new *Prosperous Soul Master Course*. In the *Master Course*, I take this material and expand it into a four-volume series with completely new components to help you master these concepts and develop your Prosperous Soul. Consider picking up my new manuals or joining my online master class where I personally cover each topic (and more) in greater detail.

I have designed the *Foundations Course* to work best in a small group setting. There are videos, lesson plans, my book *(Money and the Prosperous Soul)*, and a leader's guide to equip you on your journey as you work with friends and family at your own pace.

May you take this material and discover what God intends for you in the realm of wealth and riches. God bless your willingness to succeed, and God bless your PROSPEROUS SOUL!

HOW THIS MANUAL WORKS

This manual is designed as a workbook for my *Prosperous Soul Foundations Course*. In this manual, you will learn:

1. How your heart and mindsets play a crucial role in the success of your finances
2. How to go deeper into the spiritual aspects of money and how to align your heart and mind with heaven's economy
3. Practical tools for how to create a healthy heart that can steward and increase growth

There are a number of ways to use this manual. You can simply read through it and learn at your own pace or join in with a group. At the end of each chapter, there is a lesson overview to help you put the concepts and strategies into practice. If you're unable to tackle anything else, doing the homework at the end of each chapter will give you a basic understanding of how to become a Prosperous Soul.

The best way to use this manual is to read through it with a group using the *Prosperous Soul Foundations Course Leader's Guide*, *Money and the Prosperous Soul* book, and the *Prosperous Soul Foundations Course* video curriculum. You can get everything you need to lead or start a Prosperous Soul Group by getting the *Prosperous Soul Foundations Course* curriculum kit. There are online tools you can use as well.

Throughout this manual, you will come across different Tokens. These tokens are reminders of the work God is doing in you from each session. Collect these tokens and place them somewhere in your home or office as a reminder of what you have learned in your Prosperous Soul journey. If you do not wish to find these tokens yourself, you can pick up a Prosperous Soul Token Set online at www.stephenkdesilva.com/store.

At the end of each chapter, these categories will enrich your experience:

HOMEWORK
This section is designed to reinforce the main lessons for a Prosperous Soul. These exercises build the skeletal structure of your home finances and give you the tools necessary to think like a Prosperous Soul. (If you need extra copies of the worksheets, you can find them in the back of this book.)

VIDEO
This section shows you which videos correlate with each chapter. If there are handouts or worksheets that accompany the chapter, this section will also point you to the appropriate video tutorial to help in filling out the worksheets.

GOING DEEPER
These questions are designed to help you think more deeply, master the material, and make it more personal.

FURTHER STUDY
This section is for heavy thinkers and researchers. These books, messages, and references are where the ideas discussed in the chapter are developed further. Going through these resources will help you master this material.

PRAYER
It can be easy to leave God out of the conversation when it comes to your finances. This section has dictated prayers to help you engage with God and His heart for your finances.

PROPHETIC ACT
This section offers prophetic declarations to help activate your faith to see God's promises fulfilled in your finances. These are brief statements you can make daily. You will see a huge impact as you engage your faith with God's heart.

EXTRA RESOURCES
This section serves as a bibliography and suggested reading list. Keep in mind that this category includes material by both Christian and non-Christian authors. If you wish to study works only by Christians, feel free to ignore this section. However, reading experts in and out of the church will give you increased understanding. View it as an opportunity to practice your discernment as you "plunder Babylon" (see Hebrews 5:14).

INTRODUCTION

Welcome to the *Prosperous Soul: Foundations* manual. In the following pages, we will discover the riches woven into the apostle John's phrase "as your soul prospers."

> Beloved, I pray that in all respects you may prosper and be in good health, just as your soul prospers.
>
> 3 John 1:2

My spirit leaps at the possibilities contained in those words. Could they be the delicate thread that unravels a mystery? Could a *Prosperous Soul* be the small keyhole through which we peer? And on the other side, might we see the apostle's hope for *life more abundant?* (See John 10:10.) Could a believer's individual prosperity and health lie behind this quiet promise of a Prosperous Soul, where Christ is the key, and we are allowed to turn the lock?

We believe that Jesus completed His work on the cross and that He is the foundation of every breath and hope our lives may span. Yet, even in salvation, God does not see us as heavenly infants, helpless and dependent receivers of His kingdom bounty. Rather, we have entered a battle for His kingdom to come, His will to be done. In that battle, people's souls hang in the balance. Enough is written on taking up the armor of God. This manual is about entering the fray. It is about spiritual violence and bringing force.

> From the days of John the Baptist until now the kingdom of heaven suffers violence, and violent men take it by force.
>
> Matthew 11:12

SOMETHING DIFFERENT

Many great stewardship teachers have covered what this manual does not. I recommend their works highly and suggest you preserve a place in your personal library for their words. To aid in your study, I've included a biography following each session. From these leaders, I've gleaned the basic tools of biblical stewardship. Available to anyone wishing to gain control over their financial life, these tools are a powerful and effective message to the church. But in my experience, I've longed for something more than budget worksheets and memory verses.

As a financial counselor, I found that good information couldn't overcome bad beliefs. Though we lather a student with Scriptures and sound advice, lasting change will not happen until that student's belief system is reached. A switch must flip deep inside a person's heart, in a place where God alone can reach.

Paul tells Timothy, *"All scripture is God-breathed, effective for teaching, correction, and training in righteousness"* (2 Timothy 3:16). When a person encounters truth, that truth acts as a wave. It will continue to break against one's rocky walls of belief. In this, people choose to either harden their hearts (resist the truth) or soften, allowing the city within to change. There is no difference for believers, except we should know better than to resist. When we are faced with biblical truth, change will remain beyond our reach until we allow our walls to fall to Christ. And after biblical truth reshapes us, it is then that we rebuild our walls. We become the strong tower Solomon spoke of, for walls are not wrong in themselves.

> The name of the Lord is a strong tower; the righteous man runs into it and is safe.
>
> Proverbs 18:10

In my counseling, I had concluded that teaching alone was pointless—I needed transformative power. I desired new tools to reach our rocky walls within, in the seat of our souls. Sometimes these walls have to fall when truth washes in. Armed with techniques from Bethel's Sozo ministry, I began to piece together a unique financial deliverance ministry. What better tool, I thought, than developing a financial deliverance course that enables a person to supplant lies with biblical truth whenever God would reveal it? Enter *Prosperous Soul: Foundations*.

THE TEACHING SYSTEM

This manual is the product of many suggestions, many prayers, and many hours of study and teaching. It is designed to be a stand-alone manual, one that can be used like a textbook. Use this material to provoke study and to invite healing. May it be a gift, as we are all on the journey to become Prosperous Souls.

> Blessed be the God and Father of our Lord Jesus Christ, who according to His great mercy has caused us to be born again to a living hope through the resurrection of Jesus Christ from the dead, to obtain an inheritance which is imperishable and undefiled and will not fade away, reserved in heaven for you, who are protected by the power of God through faith for a salvation ready to be revealed in the last time. In this you greatly rejoice, even though now for a little while, if necessary, you have been distressed by various trials, so that the proof of your faith, being more precious than gold which is perishable, even though tested by fire, may be found to result in praise and glory and honor at the revelation of Jesus Christ; and though you have not seen Him, you love Him, and though you do not see Him now, but believe in Him, you greatly rejoice with joy inexpressible and full of glory, obtaining as the outcome of your faith the salvation of your souls.
>
> 1 Peter 1:3-9

Chapter 1

STEWARDSHIP

"I am a servant of Christ and a steward
of the mysteries of God. I am one found trustworthy."

TRUST

Every passage of Scripture on stewardship in the New Testament deals with the issue of trust, for *stewardship is a trust*. The more God adds to our lives, the more He trusts us. Stewardship, and everything else to which He calls us, is all about *partnership*. God wants partners who are *like Him*. He never calls us to do something without showing us how to do it Himself.

God didn't simply ask me to trust Him; He trusted me. And His trust ultimately exposed my lack of faith in Him, in myself, and in the person He said I was. But it was also His trust in me that taught me how to begin to trust Him and myself, to start thinking and acting like the son and supernatural steward He was training me to become.

Our stewardship of money (material wealth) exposes the state of our trust like nothing else, and this is why God continues to use money like the master did in the parable of the talents. Money is power, and power exaggerates whatever is in our hearts. He doesn't need us to make money for Him, and it doesn't cost Him to give us more. But it cost Him His own Son to restore us as sons and daughters who could share in His glory and His kingdom.

Only the completely faithful, the perfectly trusting, can bear the weight of that glory. This is why the most prized quality of the steward is not financial acumen, hard work, or even courage to take risks but *faithfulness* or *trustworthiness*.

> It is required of stewards that one be found trustworthy.
>
> 1 Corinthians 4:2

Jesus taught that the quality of our faithfulness can be seen in our lives no matter how small or great the issue at stake:

> He who is faithful in a very little thing is faithful also in much; and he who is unrighteous in a very little thing is unrighteous also in much.
>
> Luke 16:10

The Lord is the only One who can finally answer the question of whether or not we are being faithful; moreover, He is the only One who enables us to be faithful as Paul taught:

> Who are you to judge the servant of another? To his own master he stands or falls; and he will stand, for the Lord is able to make him stand.
>
> Romans 14:4

Take a moment and write down all the areas of your life you are stewarding. Be as complete as possible, realizing that stewardship is over more than our money. It includes our anointings, callings, and appointments, as well as the people we have been entrusted with around us.

MONEY IS POWER

Power exaggerates whatever is in our hearts, which means that we need to work from the inside out. As revival moves throughout the world, signs, wonders, and miracles will put God on display. As Prosperous Souls, we will reveal His power in our personal lives, as well as in the public displays that appear more as ministry. It is vital to recognize our role and purpose "under God" as both private and public. We will cover more about the use of power in a later chapter, but here we will discuss the need to draw the supernatural into our personal lives.

Jesus Christ said, *"You will know them by their fruits"* (Matthew 7:20). Moreover, He demonstrated the kind of fruit we are to look for—the fruit of a life lived from perfect trust in God. Christ modeled the standard of faithfulness to which we must all aspire and is thus the prime example of a believer (which we would do well to remember when we use this term to describe ourselves). He declared:

> These signs will accompany those who have believed: in My name they will cast out demons, they will speak with new tongues; they will pick up serpents, and if they drink any deadly poison, it will not hurt them; they will lay hands on the sick, and they will recover.
>
> Mark 16:17–18 (emphasis mine)

Another translation for signs that accompany is *following signs*. Notice that all of the "following signs" described by Mark involve actions—and not passive actions either, but aggressive acts against evil. Real trust in a supernatural God will manifest in this kind of supernatural behavior—Christlike behavior.

When I consider Christ's lifestyle, it strikes me that no one could describe the "signs that followed" Christ with a word like *conservative or careful.* Yes, He did instruct His disciples to pick up the leftovers after He multiplied the loaves and fishes. But such "conservation" only serves to point out that Christ ministered out of extravagant generosity and abundance. This is the kind of supernatural stewardship that flows from a heart that trusts God completely and knows what God is really like—a *faithful heart.*

Review the areas of stewardship you listed earlier. Ask God to show you what your *following signs* have been for each area you listed. In this process, you should discover behaviors that are admirable and some that need improvement. For the ones that glorify God, thank Him. This is a high form of worship. For those where you have failed or struggled, ask God for forgiveness and wisdom on how to correct them. What are some ways to repent and display God in your stewardship of each area? List those ideas below.

UP-LIVING

Throughout Scripture we see that when God is with us, we are naturally supernatural. We are told in the Gospel of John that we will do greater things than these. What did Jesus mean by that statement?

Will we heal the sick and cast out demons? Will we live in divine health? Are these Scriptures for us today? The answer is an emphatic "yes." We are to do miracles, signs, and wonders. We are to base our actions upon God's Word, the absolute truth.

Many of us have had powerful experiences in our lives, some good and some bad. The ones we embrace will define our perception of reality. Our minds (the soul) build "maps" of what is true and discard as false what we don't understand. When we do this, "truth" forms around our understanding and we become in our minds the highest authority on what is true. This is the pattern Scripture calls the boastful pride of life (see 1 John 2:16).

Consider the idea of praying for the sick. Some great teachers have built entire doctrines to argue why miracles are not for today. Since they have not seen a healing or miracle, they conclude that God does not heal today. Others begin bravely enough but falter when their prayers and hopes do not seem to produce results. Pain, suffering, and death shout so loudly that the soft voice of hope is drowned out.

Some prayers appear unanswered, yet the Word of God is clear. The Bible sets the bar far above our experiences and asks us to live by faith at that high level. In spite of what we experience, we are to live with the expectation of miracles, signs, and wonders. God invites us into *up-living* in His invisible kingdom.

For a Prosperous Soul, up-living is normal. We learn to develop skills and habits to live supernaturally in both the public and private areas of our lives. In the last exercise, I asked you to list some points of repentance regarding stewardship. What patterns are emerging in your notes from earlier? In what ways are you resisting the waves of truth I discussed in the introduction? Are there areas in which you have hardened your heart? If so, ask God to help you soften your rocky walls, and allow His truth to reshape your heart. Pray this prayer:

> Father God, thank You for revealing areas of resistance to Your influence in my life. I ask You to begin to soften my heart and allow Your wisdom in Scripture to change me. I give You full access and ask for the courage now in Jesus' name. Amen.

Write down what you believe He is saying and showing you.

THE BLACK SWAN

Forming an internalized map of reality is a necessary part of being human. This mapping is a valuable tool that enables us to relate to our world and remain sane. But like most things in life, overusing any tool can become a detriment. We are not the highest authority on what is true. What we don't know can hurt us.

In his book *The Black Swan: The Impact of the Highly Improbable*, author Nassim Nicolas Taleb brilliantly describes this aspect of human nature:

> Before the discovery of Australia, people in the Old World were convinced that all swans were white, an unassailable belief as it seemed completely confirmed by empirical evidence. The sighting of the first Black Swan might have been an interesting surprise for a few ornithologists, but that is not where the significance of the story lies. It illustrates a severe limitation to our learning from observations or experience and the fragility of our knowledge. One single observation can invalidate a general statement derived from millennia of confirmatory sightings of millions of white swans. All you need is one single (and, I am told, quite ugly) black bird.[1]

So what happens to our mental maps when we see a genuine miracle? What happens when we hear or read testimonies of supernatural happenings? The miracle, the sign, and the wonder are *black swans.* These events cast new light on our perceptions of reality. They shift our paradigms of what is real. They invite us further than our experiences would take us. Believers in Jesus Christ have chosen a lifestyle of unlimited potential, a lifestyle of black swans.

---

1   Nassim Nicolas Taleb, The Black Swan: The Impact of the Highly Improbable (New York: Random House, 2007).

Because of that potential, we carry an explosive possibility into every aspect of our lives—as parents, as friends, as entrepreneurs. We can choose to live differently and lean into the miraculous. We can expect to live with a Prosperous Soul that sees the unbelievable transpire in every aspect of life. Pray this prayer:

> God, Your natural displays are black swans in my life. I ask that You would introduce Your natural displays in my life, and I would learn to first see them and then seize them. I would embrace Your supernatural lifestyle from this point forward. Make me into a supernatural steward and a Prosperous Soul. I pray this in Jesus' name. Amen.

THE RULES OF SUCCESS

God has always operated in our lives; usually the challenge lies in our recognizing His actions. And as we begin to cooperate with Him, we find our souls will prosper. This is what it looks like as we peer through the keyhole of 1 John 1:2.

A Prosperous Soul feels very much like success. In fact, they are one and the same. A friend once told me these two rules of success that his "old daddy" used to say:

1.   If you can't dream it, you can't have it.
2.   Reach out with the long arm of reality.

I saw that the first rule is designed around imagination. If we cannot "see" a good goal with the imagination, we will never reach it.

This is a reflection of how God wants us to co-labor with Him. He wants us to reach for something and not fall prey to passivity.

I found the second goal builds upon action. "The long arm of reality" reaches out and takes hold of that dream (the first rule) and drags it back into today. It requires us to act. This is a reflection of how the kingdom of heaven suffers violence and the violent take it by force.

One day, I asked my friend if there was a third rule. He laughed and replied, "Yes," but no one had asked that question before. His answer: timing.

I found the brilliance in my friend's "old daddy." The third rule of success is timing—learning not to move ahead or too far behind God's leading. Jesus is the Master of listening and seeing what Father God is doing (see John 5:19). Pray this prayer:

> God, show me how to apply the rules of success to my life, that You might call me successful.

List what you hear or see below.

THE SEVEN MOUNTAINS

There are seven mountains of influence in society; they are discussed further in chapter 5.

To take this world for the kingdom, God's servants need to scale these seven mountains because true change will not happen from the bottom but from the top. But to get to the top, we need to be prepared in our hearts to handle the power we are given.

TOKENS – STONES OF REMEMBRANCE

When the Israelites crossed the Jordan River into the Promised Land, God came to Joshua and told him to have the Israelites collect twelve stones to pile up on the other side of the river as memorial stones to remember what God did in their lives (see Joshua 4:1–8).

Collect these tokens as reminders of the work that God is doing in you from this session. Find a bag or small box to contain the tokens (there are twelve). Place these somewhere in your home or office as a reminder of what you have learned in your Prosperous Soul journey. You can also pick up a Prosperous Soul Token Set online at www.stephenkdesilva.com/store.

TOKEN 1: PENNY

Prophetically, the penny symbolizes:

First or beginning. This begins your journey of a Prosperous Soul.

Liberty is different from freedom because liberty implies the ability to choose between many possibilities, and freedom implies release or escape from a threat. A Prosperous Soul will learn to grow beyond freedom into liberty (the capacity to choose well between many opportunities). Because prosperity and riches can make a way for good and evil, a Prosperous Soul must learn personal restraint. The penny reminds us to mature in our capacity to carry liberty.

Abraham Lincoln said, "Any man can withstand adversity. If you wish to test a man's character, give him power."

The motto of the United States: In God We Trust. This speaks of the need to trust in God, not money.

God created us to use our imaginations and to dream. Dreaming connects us to vision. Imagine Paul's phrase *"Far more abundantly beyond."* What do you think that means? What possibilities could emerge if that phrase manifested in your life? Read the following verse aloud as a prophetic declaration over your life. Then read it aloud again, making it first person. Replace "we" and "us" with "I" and "me." Pay attention to how the declaration *feels* when you say it with faith.

> Now to Him who is able to do far more abundantly beyond all that we ask or think, according to the power that works within us...
>
> Ephesians 3:20

Imagine this verse manifesting in your life. Ask God to give you a prophetic picture of what that might mean. Read the verse aloud one more time, only this time, write down what God is showing you.

Choose one of the things you listed above and dream about it for a moment. What would it look like in your life if it manifested? What would it feel like if God were to ask you to steward it for the rest of your life? Remember the first rule of success? "If you can't dream it, you can't have it." Take a moment to dream about it. Write down your impressions and discoveries in this exercise.

I CANNOT FIND MY DREAM

Many of us find that imagining good things in our lives may be too hard because of difficult experiences or lack of hope. Some have even been taught that dreaming and redeemed imaginations are wrong or dangerous. Such an idea is contrary to Scripture and will ultimately rob a person's creativity. If you are unsure, here is a Scripture to meditate upon:

> Where there is no vision, the people are unrestrained, but happy is he who keeps the law.
>
> Proverbs 29:18

I found that relighting the fire to dream is key to an emerging Prosperous Soul. Though the loss of that fire is an epidemic among God's people, He is again passing a torch over us for the very purpose of reignition. Those who have lost the capacity to dream have likely had their trust in God seriously damaged; the inability to dream is a crisis of trust. This section will begin to rebuild your fundamental appetite for trusting in God. Following is a chart of enemy schemes showing how the enemy causes people to stop dreaming. These headings are Toil, Fear, and Sabotage, which describe three broad strategies the devil uses to extinguish a person's dreams.

The category called "Sounds Like" identifies the enemy's declaration over you according to the scheme. How deeply we are convinced by the scheme will determine how loudly and regularly we find ourselves parroting, "I'm too busy" or "I'm too tired." The category called "Feels Like" identifies the symptomatic emotions that accompany the scheme. Finally, the category called "Remedy" offers the powerful biblical solution.

I will devote the remainder of this chapter to discussing elements on the first row entitled Toil (Evil One).

Enemy Schemes	Sounds Like...	Feels Like...	Remedy
Toil (Evil One) Ex: Cain, Martha Ref: 1 John 3:12	Too busy Too tired Too hard	Inconvenience Drudgery Discouragement Impatience	Sabbath
Fear (Punishment) Ex: Saul (1 Sam. 15:24) Ref: 1 John 4:18	I am afraid I will fail It will hurt I am insecure	Double-mindedness Insecurity/Suspicion Lack of control Insignificance Slavery/Fear of man	Adoption Rom. 8:15
Sabotage (Betrayal) Ex: Joseph Ref: Gen. 50:20	Threats Warnings Abandonment	Trauma Victimization Hopelessness	Courage Vision

The second row entitled Fear (Punishment) is discussed in chapter 4. The third row entitled Sabotage (Betrayal) is discussed in chapter 5. Remember, the goal of the enemy is to extinguish a believer's capacity to dream and imagine. I encourage you to complete this chapter and participate in the following exercises on dreaming even if you feel that fear or sabotage is not something you struggle with.

EVIL ONE

Many people live an excessively busy lifestyle. Several years ago, I was a textbook example, working seven-day weeks as the comptroller of Bethel Church and running my own CPA practice on evenings and weekends. Though I began with noble intentions, my servant lifestyle grew unbearable with drudgery. Near utter exhaustion, I had crossed the blurry boundary between trusting in God and trusting in my own strength.

Hebrews 4:12 says that "*the word of God is living and active and…able to judge the thoughts and intentions of the heart.*" Owning my need for wisdom, I was leafing through 1 John when I found a reference to the "evil one."

> We know that no one who is born of God sins; but He who was born of God keeps him, and the evil one does not touch him. We know that we are of God, and that the whole world lies in the power of the evil one.
>
> 1 John 5:18–19

Finding my *Strong's Concordance*, I looked up the definition of the word *evil*. Expecting to find a reference akin to devils or demons, I was surprised by this Greek word meaning *to toil, toilsome,* or *bad*. God was showing me that my overwork was not from Him, that it had become an evil in my life. Using the New American Standard Version, I looked up every verse where this "evil one" phrase was used. Here are the verses (with emphasis added), all in the New Testament and all using the same Greek word meaning to toil:

When anyone hears the word of the kingdom and does not understand it, the evil one comes and snatches away what has been sown in his heart. This is the one on whom seed was sown beside the road.

Matthew 13:19

And the field is the world; and as for the good seed, these are the sons of the kingdom; and the tares are the sons of the evil one.

Matthew 13:38

I do not ask You to take them out of the world, but to keep them from the evil one.

John 17:15

In addition to all, taking up the shield of faith with which you will be able to extinguish all the flaming arrows of the evil one.

Ephesians 6:16

But the Lord is faithful, and He will strengthen and protect you from the evil one.

2 Thessalonians 3:3

I am writing to you, fathers, because you know Him who has been from the beginning. I am writing to you, young men, because you have overcome the evil one. I have written to you, children, because you know the Father.

1 John 2:13

Not as Cain, who was of the evil one and slew his brother. And for what reason did he slay him? Because his deeds were evil, and his brother's were righteous.

1 John 3:12

We knew that no one who is born of God sins; but He who was born of God keeps him, and the evil one does not touch him.

1 John 5:18

We know that we are of God, and that the whole world lies in the power of the evil one.

1 John 5:19

If we study these verses with the understanding that "evil one" means toil, toilsome, or bad, we can begin to get a new perspective on the enemy's plan. Read each of the "evil one" verses aloud, substituting the phrase "evil one" with the word *toil*. Write down any thoughts you sense from the Holy Spirit.

God was showing me how the enemy had crept into my life through excessive busyness. The Lord was answering my prayers by revealing the boundary between trust in Him and trust in human strength. This isn't new or unique to my story; consider Solomon's wisdom on blessings:

> It is the blessing of the Lord that makes rich, and He adds no sorrow to it.

Proverbs 10:22

Or Jesus' answer to Martha:

> But Martha was distracted with all her preparations; and she came up to Him and said, "Lord, do You not care that my sister has left me to do all the serving alone? Then tell her to help me." But the Lord answered and said to her, "Martha, Martha, you are worried and bothered about so many things; but only one thing is necessary, for Mary has chosen the good part, which shall not be taken away from her."

Luke 10:40-42

Ask God to speak to you about your own life and to show you if the enemy's fingerprints are around you. Consider whether toil has affected your life. Write down your discoveries

My revelation for toil resulted in a prompt and passionate cry for God to show me the remedy. God's answer to this problem came quickly; the next day He clearly spoke these three words: "Keep My Sabbath."

SABBATH IS FOR TODAY

Until this directive, Sabbath for me had remained a cryptic old law that was good but somehow expired by the advent of Christ in the New Testament. I subtly believed that Jesus was a Sabbath breaker; if that was good enough for Him, it was good enough for me.

> But the synagogue official, indignant because Jesus had healed on the Sabbath, began saying to the crowd in response, "There are six days in which work should be done; so come during them and get healed, and not on the Sabbath day."
>
> Luke 13:14

Of course, my naiveté concerning the Sabbath had no relevance to the noble intentions of Jesus as He healed on that day. I began to study *Sabbath* and found that the Sabbath continued after the cross and into the new church.

> The next Sabbath nearly the whole city assembled to hear the word of the Lord.
>
> Acts 13:4

Further, Jesus did not come to eliminate the Sabbath but to fulfill it.

> Do not think that I came to abolish the Law or the Prophets; I did not come to abolish but to fulfill.
>
> Matthew 5:17

Finally, He Himself has become the Sabbath rest.

> So there remains a Sabbath rest for the people of God. For the one who has entered His rest has himself also rested from his works, as God did from His. Therefore let us be diligent to enter that rest, so that no one will fall, through following the same example of disobedience.
>
> Hebrews 4:9–11

These verses converge to illustrate our role in resting in Christ—bringing us back to trusting in God. The enemy's scheme to lure us into extreme busyness will serve to blur that line of trusting in God. Left unattended, we will find ourselves exhausted, discouraged, and toiling, our capacity to dream extinguished.

God takes the Sabbath so seriously that an entire nation's captivity remained *"until the land had enjoyed its Sabbaths."*

> Those who had escaped from the sword he carried away to Babylon; and they were servants to him and to his sons until the rule of the kingdom of Persia, to fulfill the word of the Lord by the mouth of Jeremiah, until the land had enjoyed its Sabbaths. All the days of its desolation it kept Sabbath until seventy years were complete.
>
> 2 Chronicles 36:20–21

The conditions for Sabbath are simple, but the implications are profound. To complete my own story, I was forced by faith into a violent act. Tearing a hole in my seven-day workweek, I began a weekly Sabbath rest. It was an example of taking the kingdom of heaven by force (see Matthew 11:12) when I allowed work to wait and I began to rest on one day each week. It was not easy, but it was miraculous to watch God grow my business even further as weeks became years and He proved Himself faithful.

See, the Lord has given you the Sabbath; therefore He gives you bread for two days on the sixth day. Remain every man in his place; let no man go out of his place on the seventh day.

Exodus 16:29

Toil attacks your capacity to dream by wearing you down and keeping you too busy. It replaces your enthusiasm with discouragement. God created us to use our imaginations and to dream because dreaming connects us to His purpose for our lives. Imagine what "abundantly beyond" could mean. What limits could it remove in your life?

Now to Him who is able to do far more abundantly beyond all that we ask or think, according to the power that works within us...

Ephesians 3:20

TOKEN 2: GLASS BEAD

Prophetically, the glass bead symbolizes:

Reawakening the dreamer in you (see Genesis 37:19)

The first rule of success: *if you can't dream it, you can't have it*

Violent reaction against the scheme of the evil one (see Matthew 11:12)

"If you can't dream it, you can't have it." Turn that around—if you *can* dream it, you can have it. Go ahead and dream something. Consider it your violent act against the powers of the evil one for your own life. Hold the glass bead in your hand and pray this prayer:

Father God, I hand You disappointment, shame, and discouragement. Thank You, Papa, for what You are giving me in exchange for these things. I repent for being angry at my dreams—for blaming my dreams for my pain. And I hand to You, Father God, bad teaching that says, "See, if Joseph had just kept quiet, nothing bad would have happened to him." I break off the mindset of that teaching and replace it with the truth that those dreams actually buoyed him up in the circumstances that he was in and kept hope alive. So I repent for being mad at my dreams. I hand to You, Father God, any curse attached to being called a dreamer, and I receive back from You the ability to dream and the excitement of dreaming!

LESSONS
Chapter 1

HOMEWORK

Set aside some time and write down one hundred dreams. These dreams can be as simple as reading a novel or as challenging as writing one. The only rules are that these dreams must be yours alone and there must be one hundred.

Once you have your list of dreams, choose one and see it accomplished within one month.

VIDEO

Watch "Releasing the Dreamer (Parts I and II)" on your DVD or in the online curriculum.

GOING DEEPER

How does your stewardship with money expose or mirror your trust in God?

What does Stephen mean when he says that money is power, and power exaggerates whatever is in our hearts?

Have you ever encountered a miraculous "Black Swan" in your life?

How do you relate to Stephen's rules of success? What are some ways you can apply them to your life?

Is toil, exhaustion, or burnout a part of your life? Take 5–10 minutes to ask God if you are experiencing any of these attacks. If so, what can you do to combat their influence?

How important is it to keep God's Sabbath?
What are some ways you can start to tear holes in your schedule to keep God's rest?

FURTHER STUDY

Read *Money and the Prosperous Soul* (chapters 1 and 5).

Read or memorize 1 Corinthians 4:1–2.

Explore the subjects of Joseph (the son of Jacob), Daniel, the Evil One, and Sabbath in the Bible.

Review Tokens 1 and 2 (penny and glass bead).

PRAYER

Father God, I repent for being angry at my dreams. I ask You to reignite the dreamer within so that I can start looking beyond my circumstances and into what You're wanting to do. I hand to You, Father, any hurts or discouragement attached to dreaming, as well as any fears that I have over stewardship or money. Thank You that I am a trustworthy servant and that You have asked me to turn on my ability to dream so that I can envision Your desires and pursue them with purpose. Amen.

PROPHETIC ACT

Declare this over your life this week: "I am a servant of Christ and a steward of the mysteries of God. I am one found trustworthy."

EXTRA RESOURCES

For more information about Sozo ministry, visit www.bethelsozo.com.

For more information about the Bethel Transformation Center, visit www.ibethel.org.

For more information about Lance Wallnau's "Seven Mountains" teaching, visit www.lancelearning.com.

Book: Johnson, Bill. *Dreaming with God*. Shippensburg: Destiny Image Publishers, Inc., 2006.

Book: Johnson, Bill. *When Heaven Invades Earth*. Shippensburg: Destiny Image Publishers, Inc., 2003.

Book: Kelly, Matthew. *The Dream Manager*. Boston: Beacon Publishing, 2007.

Book: Taleb, Nassim. *The Black Swan: The Impact of the Highly Improbable*. New York: Random House, 2007.

1) Toil is first attack on dreams

Chapter 2

TROUBLE WITH MONEY

"I am faithful and a target for God's true riches."

SPIRITUAL DYNAMICS

This chapter introduces the spiritual dynamics of money, riches, and wealth. As a Prosperous Soul, one realizes that Christ can *"do far more abundantly beyond all that we ask or think, according to the power that works within us"* (see Ephesians 3:20). In the last chapter, we began to dream and use our redeemed imaginations to see what good things God may have for us. When I refer to *good things*, I'm speaking in terms of destiny and purpose, not possessions. Though God's purposes for us may include material blessings, they are not the point. Rather, a Prosperous Soul is one who is pursuing their God-given purpose—whatever it may encompass. Set your eyes on God and not on possessions.

> Do not weary yourself to gain wealth, cease from your consideration of it.
>
> Proverbs 23:4

KINGDOM STEWARDSHIP

Now that you are dreaming, let's practice. Write down what you would do if you suddenly obtained one million dollars. Write down as many activities as you can think of, attaching an estimate for each one, until the entire million is used.

Review your list above. Realize that whatever possessions God provides, you will operate consistently with your preparation and training. Understand that acquiring possessions is both an opportunity and a responsibility.

When you set your eyes on it, it is gone. For wealth certainly makes itself wings like an eagle that flies toward the heavens.

Proverbs 23:5

TOKEN 3: MILLION-DOLLAR BILL

Prophetically, the million-dollar bill symbolizes:

> The understanding that money is power, and power exaggerates whatever is in our hearts
>
> A supernatural steward's willingness to deal with the issues of the heart
>
> The steward's access to receive or possess power in the form of money, riches, and wealth
>
> The great responsibility to manage wealth for Christ with intention and wisdom

Take the token in your hand and pray the following prayer:

> Father God, I understand that money is power, and power exaggerates whatever is in my heart. I ask You to aggressively correct my perspective on money and power so that I can be found faithful. I ask for Your provision, as You see fit, for me to steward. I ask You to show me Your mysteries that I might bring You glory. May You be exaggerated in my heart. Amen.

Write down anything God may show you in this prayer.

Every believer is a steward, regardless of the size (or lack thereof) of their resources. We steward money, and we steward God-given calling, anointings, or appointments. Whether we are parents, apostles, janitors, or entrepreneurs, we are called to stewardship. Consider the depth in this verse where Paul discusses our universal call to supernatural stewardship :

> Let a man regard us in this manner, as servants of Christ and stewards of the mysteries of God.
>
> 1 Corinthians 4:1

We will be known as servants and stewards. Distilled down, this verse says that others should recognize us as servants (doers) and stewards (managers or handlers) of God's secrets. I can't imagine a more exciting promise than to have access to the secret things that God is planning.

Write down what it means to be known as a servant of Christ.

Write down what it means to be known as a steward of the mysteries of God.

JOSEPH SCHOOL OF INTENTION

Joseph was a great model of a man who stewarded the mysteries of God, successfully carrying the great responsibility of power and saving his entire nation in the process. He understood *intention*, wielding wealth as a weapon and walking powerfully and righteously beside an unrighteous king. He learned these things through challenge and training. Joseph was not born into leadership; he grew into it, co-laboring with God's given favor and his own experiences. Joseph became a Prosperous Soul.

What would you have done in Joseph's shoes? What if you were given influence, vast sums of money, or valuable ideas such as inventions and intellectual property? Looking back at your kingdom stewardship list, what will you do with the resources that God gives to you? Perhaps you are called to manage the resources until the Master returns. I call this *intention*—learning how the Master wants His estate managed while He is gone and doing it His way. Perhaps, like in the parable, He wants us to do business until He returns.

> While they were listening to these things, Jesus went on to tell a parable, because He was near Jerusalem, and they supposed that the kingdom of God was going to appear immediately. So He said, "A nobleman went to a distant country to receive a kingdom for himself, and then return. And he called ten of his slaves, and gave them ten minas and said to them, 'Do business with this until I come back.'"
>
> Luke 19:11–13

Our part of the Joseph school is to turn our challenges into understanding and to train. I believe Joseph was *trained* in Pharaoh's house. Similarly, Daniel was trained in Nebuchadnezzar's house. We should learn in advance to steward the resources God may give.

List some ideas on how you might begin (or advance) your financial stewardship education.

FINANCIAL STATISTICS

I believe financial stewardship needs to happen now. It is part of our demonstration of faithfulness to the Master. I also believe we will perform in accordance with how we have prepared. If you have prepared to give, you will give. If you have prepared to invest, you will invest. Unfortunately, most Americans prepare for wealth by consuming. When and if resources are added, they perform in accordance with their training. This has been the cause of many financial difficulties.

Today, U.S. national per capita debt is approximately $38,000 for every person (man, woman, and child) in America. That debt load has been growing an average of $3 million per day for the past two years.

Over the last twenty years, Americans have experienced increasing affluence at a level never before seen. Before today, debt was dishonorable and considered a remedy of last resort. Amounts borrowed were always to be repaid, and the norm was living without debt. Each of these ideals was considered archaic and even foolish following the consumption boom years between 1980 and 2008. Even lenders were promoting a lifestyle of living in indebtedness as a means to affluence and success.

ECONOMICS FROM GENESIS TO REVELATION

The earliest reference I have found to our modern lending banks is from ancient Mesopotamia, a region east of Abraham's Promised Land.

In Genesis, you can track Abram, who left Ur (a city in Babylonia, a region of Mesopotamia) and entered the Promised Land.

> And He said to him, "I am the Lord who brought you out of Ur of the Chaldeans, to give you this land to possess it."
>
> Genesis 15:7

God is the One who brought Abram out, giving him everywhere his foot treaded.

> You are the Lord God, who chose Abram and brought him out from Ur of the Chaldees, and gave him the name Abraham. You found his heart faithful before You, and made a covenant with him to give him the land of the Canaanite, of the Hittite and the Amorite, of the Perizzite, the Jebusite and the Girgashite—to give it to his descendants. And You have fulfilled Your promise, for You are righteous.
>
> Nehemiah 9:7-8

Abraham is the father of our faith and the one whose promises we were grafted into through Christ's sacrifice.

> Even so Abraham believed God, and it was reckoned to him as righteousness. Therefore, be sure that it is those who are of faith who are sons of Abraham. The Scripture, foreseeing that God would justify the Gentiles by faith, preached the gospel beforehand to Abraham, saying, "All the nations will be blessed in you." So then those who are of faith are blessed with Abraham, the believer.
>
> Galatians 3:6–9

Revelation explains what Abraham was delivered from: *the Babylonian system.* This is a system designed to enslave human lives. It is fascinating to me that modern lending has its roots in Babylonia, an economic system designed to enslave. And like Abraham, we have also been delivered from slavery through the cross.

> ...and cargoes of horses and chariots and slaves and human lives.
>
> Revelation 18:13

When Joseph began to sell grain, it was the Egyptians who enslaved themselves to the Babylonian system of bondage (debt).

> When that year was ended, they came to him the next year and said to him, "We will not hide from my lord that our money is all spent, and the cattle are my lord's. There is nothing left for my lord except our bodies and our lands. Why should we die before your eyes, both we and our land? Buy us and our land for food, and we and our land will be slaves to Pharaoh. So give us seed, that we may live and not die, and that the land may not be desolate." So Joseph bought all the land of Egypt for Pharaoh, for every Egyptian sold his field, because the famine was severe upon them. Thus the land became Pharaoh's.
>
> Genesis 47:18–20

This is the point of Nehemiah—that when we returned to bondage, God delivered us.

> You saw the affliction of our fathers in Egypt, and heard their cry by the Red Sea. Then You performed signs and wonders against Pharaoh, against all his servants and all the people of this land; for You knew that they acted arrogantly toward them, and made a name for Yourself as it is this day.
>
> Nehemiah 9:9-13

It was many years later that Israel fell prey to the Babylonian system. After Joseph's death and under a different pharaoh, the Jews began to suffer. It was then that God brought another deliverer for His people.

> ...until there arose another king over Egypt who knew nothing about Joseph. It was he who took shrewd advantage of our race and mistreated our fathers so that they would expose their infants and they would not survive. It was at this time that Moses was born; and he was lovely in the sight of God, and he was nurtured three months in his father's home.
>
> Acts 7:18-20

BABYLONIA

When I think of economics, I find it helpful to offer some definitions and dispel some common misconceptions. Economics is defined as the branch of knowledge concerned with the production, consumption, and transfer of wealth. It is an ancient social science with roots leading back to Mesopotamia, Greece, and Persia. Economics is not concerned with politics, but the two are nearly inseparable.

Capitalism is the economic theory with which most Americans are familiar. It is defined as an economic and political system in which a country's capital (trade and industry) is controlled by private ownership and personal gain (as opposed to state gain) from profits.

Socialism is the economic and political theory in which a country's trade and industry are controlled by the state. Private ownership and personal gain are seen as unfair concentrations of power and wealth among a small segment of society. Socialism can span a vast gamut of systems ranging from anarchism to Soviet state communism, but most European versions tend toward social democracy.

Communism is strictly a political theory derived from Karl Marx. It advocates class war and leads to a society in which all property is publicly owned.

Democracy is strictly a political theory in which the whole population is governed by representation. Both communism and democracy are beyond the scope of this manual.

However, I believe economics operate independently from the theories of capitalism and socialism. The success of both of these systems is dependent upon what Viktor Frankl calls the "race of decent man."

> From all this we may learn that there are two races of men in this world, but only these two—the "race" of the decent man and the "race" of the indecent man. Both are found everywhere; they penetrate into all groups of society. No group consists entirely of decent or indecent people.[2]

Both capitalism and socialism have strengths and weaknesses that depend upon the redemption of man. Consequently, I believe all economic theory runs upon the rails of kingdom—that of Babylonia or that of the kingdom of heaven. Thus, we find virtue and corruption in every system. Christ alone, not economic or political theory, offers a solution for systems.

---

2   Viktor E. Frankl, Man's Search for Meaning (New York: Pocket Books, 1959), 108.

Characteristics of Babylon (see Revelation 22):

> Creation and perpetuity of bondage (slavery)
>
> The view of human life as a commodity
>
> Resources are limited
>
> Artificial creation of demand (consumerism)
>
> Provision comes from human gratification

Characteristics of the kingdom of heaven:

> Commanded blessing (see Deuteronomy 28:8)
>
> Care for the poor (see Proverbs 29:7)
>
> Unmerited "fairness" (see Matthew 20:9)
>
> Lavish promotion (see Luke 19:17)
>
> Extravagant multiplication (see Matthew 13:23)
>
> Miraculous provision (see Matthew 17:27)
>
> Sow—and seed will be provided by God (see 2 Corinthians 9:10)
>
> Private ownership and accumulation (see Proverbs 13:22)

PHARAOH IS STILL DREAMING

The trouble with money today is that many people are striving for affluence and success in the absence of a Prosperous Soul. The current global economy is beginning to manifest the influence of the Babylonian system: the economic track based on the demonic motivations of sensuality, greed, and slavery in the form of consumerism and bondage.

Pharaoh (representing the world's economic leaders) has found himself in a financial nightmare. As in Abraham's time, today's soothsayers and magicians (financial pundits and sages) offer hollow interpretations. But out of bondage will rise many, perhaps thousands, of Josephs—men and women who are here to explain the dreams and lay out God's course for the future. And, like Abraham, we have come upon yet another colossal shift in the world's wealth.

Jesus qualified us for Abraham's promises; He made us to be a free people in His kingdom economy. We are called to steward the mysteries of God. This is larger than merely debt freedom. It includes all the attributes above of His economy and more.

> Let a man regard us in this manner, as servants of Christ and stewards of the mysteries of God.
>
> 1 Corinthians 4:1

Place your hand on your head and declare, "I am a Prosperous Soul." Ask the Holy Spirit to show you steps to take to correct your own private troubles with money. For example, He may ask you to get out of debt or to give more. Perhaps He wants you to take a basic financial course. I encourage your involvement with the extra resources section in the chapter 2 lesson overview.

LESSONS
Chapter 2

HOMEWORK

Choose an outstanding bill or credit card account and design a plan to pay it off completely within the shortest reasonable period. As part of your plan, create room for small celebrations along the way until the balance is paid in full. Examples of celebrations may be treating yourself to an excellent dinner out or buying something you have had to wait for.

Ask God for grace and favor with your plan, and stick to it for one month. At the end of the month, seriously consider how you feel about your progress, and set your sights on paying off the remaining debt in your life.

VIDEO

Watch videos "Trouble with Money (Parts I and II)" on your DVD or in the online curriculum.

GOING DEEPER

How would you describe your current perspective on debt?

How does viewing debt as bondage change your attitude toward finances?

What are five things you can start, five things you can stop, and five things you can change to take ownership of your possessions?

In what ways have you seen the Babylonian system and debt ruin peoples' lives?

In your opinion, how is the church combatting or contributing toward the perpetuation of the Babylonian system?

How has consumerism or "affluenza" affected your life or the lives of others?

Spend 5–10 minutes dreaming about what it would be like to be debt free. What goals could you accomplish? What unique places could you visit?

FURTHER STUDY

Read *Money and the Prosperous Soul* (chapter 2).

Read or memorize Proverbs 27:23–27.

Explore the subjects of Babylon, debt, and borrowing in the Bible.

Review Token 3 (million-dollar bill).

PRAYER

Father God, I ask for grace as I transition from a Babylonian mindset to a kingdom economy. I ask that You protect my finances and give me strategies so that I can combat debt while pursuing Your calling. I hand to You, Father, any fears over debt and thank You, Lord, that You are much bigger than any economic system that could try to enslave me. Thank You that I am trustworthy and am able to position myself in Your new, heavenly economy. I ask this all in Jesus' name. Amen.

PROPHETIC ACT

Declare this week, "I am faithful and a target for God's true riches."

EXTRA RESOURCES

Prosperous Home: A Basic Guide to Budgeting and Money Management Volume 1 at www.stephenkdesilva.com/store.

Begin a personal budget program using the software of your choice.

For the latest calculator on U.S. national debt, go to www.brillig.com/debt_clock.

Book: Bolz, Shawn. *Keys to Heaven's Economy: An Angelic Visitation from the Minister of Finance.* North Sutton, NH: Streams Publishing House, 2005.

Book: Burkett, Larry. D*ollars and Sense: Bible Wisdom for the Faithful Steward.* Uhrichsville: Barbour Books, 1993.

Book: Clason, George S. T*he Richest Man in Babylon: The Success Secrets of the Ancients.* New York: Signet, 1955.

Book: Dayton, Howard. *Your Money Counts.* Crown Ministries by Tyndale House Publishers, 1996.

Book: Hancock, Maxine. *Living on Less and Liking It More.* Wheaton: Victor Books, 1994.

Book: *Redding & Shasta County: Gateway to the Cascades.* Windsor Publications, Inc., 1986: (27).

Book: Ramsey, Dave. *The Total Money Makeover: A Proven Plan for Financial Fitness.*

Chapter 3

SPIRIT OF POVERTY

"Poverty is not my friend,
and I am a prospering child of God."

AS A MAN THINKS

The Bible is clear about the potency of our thoughts. A poverty spirit can become our view of the world. It can become our paradigm, an expectation of evil.

A poverty paradigm can be described as an attitude or "bent." The word bent literally means "to hang" (see Hosea 11:7). Any bent toward poverty is a hang-up, which needs to be straightened (removed).

Consider the word spirit. In Scripture, *spirit* usually comes from *ruach* (Hebrew) and *pneuma* (Greek), meaning breath, wind, or spirit.

The word *breath* implies life or alive. The word *wind* implies the strength within a living creature. The word *spirit* sometimes implies an attitude or a perspective. Understand that spirits of slavery, oppression, deception, etc. are not demons but attitudes that we hold. We must tune out what we are listening to and tune in to the virtues of God. A beggarly attitude causes us to tune in to the broadcast of the poverty spirit. We need to tune back in to the virtues that God announces.

VIRTUES OF THE KINGDOM

There is more than enough in the kingdom of God. Remember, too, that God is in a good mood. These statements are examples of virtues that God broadcasts, which the Prosperous Soul can tune in to.

Understand that though a person may despise poverty, they could continue to hold on to the poverty mindset (beggarly attitude). In spite of the destructive nature of the spirit of poverty, a person owns it. Some will even fight to keep themselves down and will attempt to pull down those who are trying to climb out. Poverty is possessive.

Scripture highlights the possessive nature of poverty:

> Your poverty will come in like a vagabond and your need like an armed man.
>
> Proverbs 6:11 (emphasis mine)

Let him drink and forget his poverty and remember his trouble no more.

Proverbs 31:7 (emphasis mine)

There are several stories of athletes and celebrities who earn large amounts of money and propel themselves into places of power and influence. Unfortunately, many display their inability to handle the power associated with that money and ultimately end up destroying their lives.

POVERTY ATTACKS YOUR DREAMS

The possessive nature of the spirit of poverty despises success and attacks dreams and redeemed imaginations of success. Joseph went through tremendous suffering but held on to his dream.

Sometimes we blame Joseph's struggle on the dream, but that is not accurate. Rather, the poverty spirit in other people led to Joseph's suffering. The dream served as a buoy throughout Joseph's life, lifting him out of his troubles.

Often believers are tempted to hide their dreams for fear that people or circumstances will turn against them. In truth, it is the dream that riveted Joseph's vision and fueled his courage in the face of overwhelming challenges.

POVERTY SPIRIT DEFINED

You have probably heard the phrase "poverty spirit" or "spirit of poverty." Perhaps you have heard someone describe a person, a community, or a nation as having a "poverty spirit." Or perhaps you have been in a prayer meeting where the spirit of poverty was bound, rebuked, or cast down. Such prayers understandably give rise to the idea of a "demon of poverty" that inhabits homes and regions and national identities. If this were the case, then ending poverty would be a simple matter of casting the demon of poverty out according to Jesus' command in Matthew 10:8. But deliverance alone is not enough to end poverty. While the spirit of poverty does involve demonic influence, there is more to it than that.

The basic message of poverty is this: *there is never enough.* And when people live long under the influence of this message, it takes on a personal tone: *there is never enough for you because you aren't worth it.* As you can see, the message of lack attacks you at the deepest level of your identity, value, and purpose. Poverty is not an economic problem; it is a soul and spirit problem. Lack in any area of our lives, whether our basic needs (like food, clothing, and shelter) or our more complex needs (like opportunities, friendship, affection, and knowledge), *bends* the soul and spirit.

Once a person has been bent by a poverty spirit, they may eventually overcome areas of lack but still retain that bent in their soul.

Because a poverty paradigm is rooted in our core beliefs about ourselves and the world, it has a very powerful hold. Proverbs 23:7 speaks to this power: *"For as he thinks within himself, so he is."*

The paradigm that guides our thinking is actually creating and perpetuating our reality. That is, our habits of mind define our habits of life. And as creatures of habit, one of the most difficult things for humans to do is to question the reality in which these habits work.

We will never overcome the influence of poverty until we learn to become stewards of what we listen to. This is why Jesus instructed us to be vigilant about our "hearing."

> Take care what you listen to. By your standard of measure it will be measured to you; and more will be given you besides.
>
> Mark 4:24

Bill Johnson explains the difference between listening and hearing:

> When we listen, we allow what we are hearing to gain our attention and focus, which in turn influences our beliefs and values. These beliefs and values set a standard for our ears that ultimately determines the voices that we pick up in our environment.[3]

If we have allowed the message of poverty to set the standard for our ears, then we will hear that message all around us. It is like tuning in to a radio frequency. This is similar to the description Francis Frangipane gives of a demonic power, which is one of the demonic entities Paul lists in Ephesians 6:12. In his book *The Three Battlegrounds*, Frangipane explains that a power is an evil energy that broadcasts lies like radio waves over a territory.

---

3   Bill Johnson, Strengthen Yourself in the Lord (Shippensburg: Destiny Image Publishers, Inc., 2007).

Frangipane goes on to explain that powers are not cast out, but they are displaced by the full reign of Christ in the church and through prayer.[4]

If we think of poverty as a radio station that broadcasts the lie of lack, then the principle of displacement works something like this—we create new channels of virtue (truth found in the Bible about Christ and His heavenly economy) and broadcast the truth. We put the enemy out of business, eventually starving him out of customers, with the powerful truth of Jesus Christ's message. We refuse the poverty message and invite others to tune him out also. But displacement isn't complete if we simply tune the enemy out. We must choose to tune in to a different message. We change the channel.

TOKEN 4: PAIR OF DIMES

Prophetically, the two dimes symbolize:

> A paradigm (pair of dimes) shift from the poverty spirit to a Prosperous Soul (see Colossians 1:13)

> Ten or tenth stands for our living sacrifice to God (see Romans 12:1).

> Sanctification and purification (see Hebrews 10:10)

Place two dimes between your thumb and forefinger. Slide them around and consider how easily they slip over each other. Declare that your paradigm will slip as easily as these dimes as God displaces poverty thinking with a Prosperous Soul. Pray the following prayer:

> Father God, my life is Yours, held in Your hand by Your will and Christ's authority. I offer my life to You as a living sacrifice and ask that You transfer my thinking from the influences of a poverty spirit to the blessings that follow a Prosperous Soul. I pray this in Jesus' name. Amen.

Place your hand on your head and declare: "By God's grace and my cooperation with His Holy Spirit, I am a Prosperous Soul."

---

4   Francis Frangipane, The Three Battlegrounds (Cedar Rapids: Arrow Publishing, 1989).

PERSONS, COMMUNITIES, NATIONS

Many of us are familiar with the effects of the poverty spirit over a person or a nation (parts of Africa, for example) but may be unsure of how it affects a community. For such an example, I need look no further than my hometown. Redding was known as Poverty Flats back in the 1800s. Over the generations, our city accumulated a strong faith community but continued to struggle economically.

Churches were strong separately but had little interactive cooperation. Because the poverty spirit attacks generosity, Pastor Bill Johnson went on the offensive and collected an offering for other churches in the area. The gifts began a chain reaction among these other churches, initiating giving between them and striking a critical blow at the roots of poverty.

This strategy serves as an example of how the poverty spirit reigns over a geographic area, and generosity is a key to displacing this spiritual power. I believe this was vital in the transformation of the city into an open heaven.

DISPLACING POWERS

We displace a poverty spirit (rather than cast it out), regardless of whether it is found in a person, community, or nation. Tuning in to truth from the Bible, we resist the temptation to cooperate with poverty lies.

The apostle Paul was addressing the same thing when he taught the church how to wage war in the spiritual realm.

> For the weapons of our warfare are not of the flesh, but divinely powerful for the destruction of fortresses. We are destroying speculations and every lofty thing raised up against the knowledge of God, and we are taking every thought captive to the obedience of Christ.
>
> 2 Corinthians 10:4-5

POVERTY SPIRIT	PROSPEROUS SOUL
Creates anxiety	Anxious for nothing
Passive	Perseverance
Afraid of God	Confident in God
Stress overwhelms	Stress brings grace
Hoarding	Conserving
Victim of circumstance	Significance
Instant gratification	Self-control
You serve money	Money serves you
Feelings of fear	Feelings of contentment
You are provider	God is provider
Mistakes are permanent	Mistakes are temporary
Feelings of invisibility	Apple of God's eye
Can't afford to give	Can't afford to withhold
Held back and demoted	Advanced and promoted

Take a moment and study the chart above. Consider how the poverty spirit has influence over you. Create your own list of effects you may recognize as the poverty spirit working in your life. It will be easy to recognize these influences as they will display a possessive theme, trying to hold you back, pull you down, keep you from dreaming and success. Ask God to reveal these things, and write down what you learn.

Declare Romans 8:15 over yourself. Ask God to plant it into your heart.

> For you have not received a spirit of slavery leading to fear again, but you have received a spirit of adoption as sons by which we cry out, "Abba! Father!"

BREAKING THE POVERTY SPIRIT

Finally, we will break the stronghold of the poverty spirit over your life using a simple but powerful prophetic symbol—a common paper clip.

TOKEN 5: PAPER CLIP

Prophetically, the paper clip symbolizes:

The circular, possessive nature of the poverty spirit

The poverty spirit's design to hold you

Bents in your life toward a beggarly attitude

STRAIGHTENING ATTITUDES

With the idea of a bent in mind, take a common paper clip and straighten it out using your fingers. Getting it as straight as possible, you will see there are spots where the old bends remain.

A *bent* describes a leaning toward a certain thing or a tendency toward something. You have to straighten the bent or tendency toward wrong, powerless thinking and acting, which in turn will break the spirit of poverty in your life.

Take the straightened wire in your hands and begin to bend it over and over. Continue this bending back and forth until the wire is broken. As you work at this representation of the poverty spirit, pray this prayer:

> Father God, I recognize bents in my life toward poverty thinking. I ask now that You would invade my heart, that You would invade my mind, with the truth of the gospel and displace the lies of poverty. I break this wire now as a prophetic symbol of poverty thinking, in Jesus' name, and I pray that it would be an example of the broken poverty spirit in my thinking for all my days and the days of my children and the days of all my legacy. I pray this in Jesus' name. Amen.

If the wire will not break, find some pliers or bend the wire into loops for a better grip. Continue until it is broken and throw one half into a garbage can. The other half can be kept with your other tokens as a memorial of this victory.

Finally, place your hand on your head and declare, "I am a Prosperous Soul."

LESSONS
Chapter 3

HOMEWORK

Plan a purchase. Choose something that will become a symbol in your home and be of a noticeably higher quality than what you would normally buy. Delay your purchase until you have accumulated enough excess cash to buy it; you cannot use credit. Place the new item in an obvious place in your home.

VIDEO

Watch "Spirit of Poverty (Parts I and II)" on your DVD or in the online curriculum.

GOING DEEPER

Describe poverty in your own words.

How does seeing poverty as a mindset rather than a demon change your perspective on it?

Are any of poverty's "fingerprints" present in your life?

What are some steps you can take to "tune out" poverty's broadcasts?

How does poverty attack your dreams?

What is God's heart for money? What is His solution for poverty?

FURTHER STUDY

Read *Money and the Prosperous Soul* (chapter 3).

Read or memorize Deuteronomy 28:11–12.

Explore the subjects of spirit, bent, poverty, prosper, and prosperity in the Bible.

Review Tokens 4 and 5 (pair of dimes and paper clip).

PRAYER

Father God, I recognize bents in my life toward poverty thinking. I ask now that You would invade my heart with the truth of the gospel and displace any lies of poverty. I pray that my house would be an example of healthy prosperity and that the days of my children's children will be filled with blessing. I pray this in Jesus' name. Amen.

PROPHETIC ACT

Declare this over your finances: "Poverty is not my friend, and I am a prospering child of God."

EXTRA RESOURSES

CD: Johnson, Bill. "A Key to Revival." (Recorded at Dayspring in Castle Hill, Australia, March 2004). www.ibethel.org/store.

CD: Johnson, Bill. "Generosity: A Military Move." (Recorded at Bethel in November 1999). www.ibethel.org/store.

Book: Frangipane, Francis. *The Three Battlegrounds*. Cedar Rapids: Arrow Publishing, 1989.

Book: Johnson, Bill. *Strengthen Yourself in the Lord.* Shippensburg: Destiny Image Publishers, Inc., 2007.

Book: Vallotton, Kris. *The Supernatural Ways of Royalty*. Shippensburg: Destiny Image Publishers, Inc., 2005.

Chapter 4

ROOT OF TRUTH

*"With God's help, I am tending the garden
of my heart. Lies I have believed are being removed,
and biblical truth is being planted."*

FEAR AND THE CHART OF ENEMY SCHEMES

Below you will find the Chart of Enemy Schemes from chapter 1. As promised, we will look into the scheme of Fear.

Enemy Schemes	Sounds Like...	Feels Like...	Remedy
Toil (Evil One) Ex: Cain, Martha Ref: 1 John 3:12	Too busy Too tired Too hard	Inconvenience Drudgery Discouragement Impatience	Sabbath
Fear (Punishment) **Ex: Saul (1 Sam. 15:24)** **Ref: 1 John 4:18**	**I am afraid** **I will fail** **It will hurt** **I am insecure**	**Double-mindedness** **Insecurity/Suspicion** **Lack of control** **Insignificance** **Slavery/Fear of man**	**Adoption** **Rom. 8:15**
Sabotage (Betrayal) Ex: Joseph Ref: Gen. 50:20	Threats Warnings Abandonment	Trauma Victimization Hopelessness	Courage Vision

Fear, defined as the expectation of punishment, is the opposite of faith, which is the expectation of reward. Fear is a root that grows from some seed other than love. Fear is faith in the ill will of God.

> There is no fear in love; but perfect love casts out fear, because fear involves punishment, and the one who fears is not perfected in love.
>
> 1 John 4:18

And without faith it is impossible to please Him, for he who comes to God must believe that He is and that He is a rewarder of those who seek Him.

Hebrews 11:6

In the last chapter, we discussed the spiritual weapon of displacement. Key to the success of displacement is the need to fill the resulting vacuum with biblical truth. This chapter will show you how to "pull weeds and plant flowers" in the garden of your heart.

The poverty spirit will allow many lies to grow in our hearts, and that growth is the cause of a beggarly attitude. One example of a poverty-spirit lie is fear. Fear of punishment or pain is a great de-motivator of dreamers and redeemed imaginers.

BELIEVING AND BECOMING

Many people ascribe their success or failure to the words spoken over them as children. A parent or a coach makes a passing comment that "sticks." From there, words act like seeds that take root and slowly grow into identity over the course of a lifetime. First, like a sapling, tender ideas are flexible. But with reinforcement, they grow wooden. Stiff and fixed like a tree, these ideas grow complex and broad enough to carry entire structures.

They bear fruit in the form of behaviors and patterns that others observe as character (or perhaps the lack thereof). If these originating seeds are good and affirming, the tree can grow strong and become a sanctuary for others. This is where great leaders come from. If these seeds are destructive and damaging, the tree can still grow strong. However, the resulting detrimental behaviors and habits recreate the same around themselves. Regardless, the tree will be productive, bearing fruit after its own kind. This is the promise of Scripture, from the very foundations of mankind.

Then God said, "Let the earth sprout vegetation: plants yielding seed, and fruit trees on the earth bearing fruit after their kind with seed in them"; and it was so. The earth brought forth vegetation, plants yielding seed after their kind, and trees bearing fruit with seed in them, after their kind; and God saw that it was good.

Genesis 1:11–12

This section of Genesis repeats the phrase *"after their kind"* for every element of creation, and people are no exception to this spiritual law. We bear fruit after our own kind. This is the basis of inheritance—the passing on of one's nature, from us to our children, regardless of our intent. The good news is that "it is good" according to God and that we can change the seeds.

RECOGNIZING TRUTH

Begin with the idea that words and ideas are seeds, and those seeds from the past have been sown into the garden of our hearts. Whether good or bad, these seeds will root if we allow ourselves to believe in the validity of what we're being told.

We all know how common it is to find stories of harm and pain. We also know that we can form "truth" around our experiences, permanently enshrining them in our souls, which is how we keep a grasp on reality. We learn to *trust* in what we hear and see. This "truth" moves beyond memory or experience and becomes *identity*. From this identity, we act and behave in ways that are consistent with our beliefs.

We are made in God's image, and because of this, we are capable of creating our realities. Consequently, many external realities form out of our internal truths.

> **Spiritual Principle:** We become what we believe to be true about ourselves (see Proverbs 23:7 and Romans 10:10).

Seeds are placed in our lives continually, but the ones we embrace with agreement will form our internal truth. And what we believe in will determine our actions. What is in our hearts will be produced in our lives.

Jesus referred to this spiritual principle in Matthew 7. Here He is warning us of false prophets and false teachers. He explains that their behaviors are like fruit in the way that fruit exposes the nature of the tree. In Luke, we find that this is always the case.

For there is no good tree which produces bad fruit, nor, on the other hand, a bad tree which produces good fruit. For each tree is known by its own fruit. For men do not gather figs from thorns, nor do they pick grapes from a briar bush. The good man out of the good treasure of his heart brings forth what is good; and the evil man out of the evil treasure brings forth what is evil; for his mouth speaks from that which fills his heart.

Luke 6:43-45

A good tree will bear good fruit; a bad tree will bear bad fruit. Applying this to our lives, we see that things we believe to be true will bear fruit consistent with the nature of the seed that produced that fruit. In other words, if we believe a lie, it will produce only bad fruit. Likewise, if we believe in something true to Scripture, it will produce only good fruit.

Bad behavioral or financial decisions come from seeds of what we have believed. If those bad seeds have grown into trees in our lives, they will be a source of bad behaviors.

Unless you cut the roots, you cannot stop a bad tree from producing bad fruit. At the beginning of time God set up the *after their kind* principle (see Genesis 1).

It is our responsibility to root out lies that have settled in our hearts. When we replace the lies with the truth from the Word of God, we will once again produce healthy fruit.

CREATING FROM THE INSIDE

We are created in God's image, and therefore we create the environment around us from what is inside of us.

These signs will accompany [follow] those who have believed...

Mark 16:17

Jesus revealed a spiritual principle that behaviors and actions will always follow what a person believes. *"You will know them by their fruits."* Because of this principle, we are able to look at our behaviors as indicators of what seeds are planted in our hearts. Bad behaviors result from lies that have rooted and borne fruit.

Good behaviors are the same way. So this chapter deals with interpreting behaviors, exposing destructive lies, and repenting of their influence. This is the exercise of integrity.

TOKEN 6: MUSTARD SEEDS

Prophetically, the seeds symbolize:

Ideas, which are seeds able to reproduce themselves

Truth formed when we believe ideas, whether those ideas are good or evil

The creative power in us to create the environment around us from what is inside

The actions we take based upon what we believe to be true

Place the seeds in your hand and pray the following prayer:

Holy Spirit, I want You to search me and reveal to me the wounds and lies attached to my spirit. Enable me to recognize the roots of my bad behaviors so I can sever those roots and be free. Place new truth in those places and bless them that I would flourish as a Prosperous Soul. I pray this in Jesus' name. Amen.

Write down lies in your life that result in bad behaviors. Follow each one with a replacing truth and surrender them to the Lord.

When you complete your list, pray this prayer:

Father God, I recognize the fruit of failure and evil in my life—distortions and addictions, shortfalls and failures. I ask You now to anoint me to pull up from the roots all of these lies. I remove these lies and I do it in Jesus' name. Holy Spirit, anoint me now as I remove every lie that has bound me.

I forgive anyone in the prior generations who opened a door to these seeds. As I forgive, I ask You, Jesus, to break my family free from any generational roots.

Father God, I know the good seed of truth is found in Your Word. Anoint my hands again now and plant that truth in my heart. Make Your truth penetrate the very fabric of my life.

I love Your life. I love serving You. I love being Your child. I know Your truth is real and I give You my heart. God, I ask that You would produce plentiful fruit from this good seed, as we supplant the lies of my life with the truth of the gospel. Thank You, Jesus.

Thank You, Father God, that You always trade up. There are some things on this list that I have believed are my identity, but they are less than I am called to be. So, as I lay those down, I know that You will give more than what I give to You. Today I'm asking for an identity change.

Take a moment and write down everything the Holy Spirit says about you and whatever He may say He wants to plant in place of these old lies.

This exercise may need to be repeated several times. As a help to identify lies, consider reviewing the Curious List of Lies in appendix C. If any of these lies relate to you, repeat this exercise until the Holy Spirit releases you.

LESSONS
Chapter 4

HOMEWORK

Choose an entire day and keep a Sabbath. Ask God to help you rest. Fill your time with simple activities, relationships, and creativity. Do this one-day-per-week rest for a full month, after which you may choose to continue it as a new part of your busy life. Keep a journal of your Sabbath experiences.

VIDEO

Watch "Roots of Trust" on your DVD or in the online curriculum.

GOING DEEPER

How does "picking off fruit" rather than "digging up the roots" contribute to the problem?

Israel wandered in the desert for forty years because their internal reality (of slavery) manifested in their external reality. What are some of your internal realities that are keeping you back from breakthrough?

Ask God to begin to reveal any lies you are believing and then pray with God to uproot their influence.

What are your thoughts on trust? Is there a lie or "half truth" you are trusting more than God?

What truths can you use to combat the enemy's lies?

FURTHER STUDY

Read *Money and the Prosperous Soul* (chapter 4).

Read or memorize Luke 6:43–45.

Explore the subjects of adoption, fear, and double-mindedness in the Bible.

Review Token 6 (mustard seed).

PRAYER

Thank You, Father God, for always trading up. I hand to You any lies I am believing about myself, others, and You. I lay the lies at the feet of Your Son's cross and ask for Your truth to be revealed and put in their place. Help me to hold on to these truths so that I can produce healthy, lasting fruit. I pray this all in Jesus' name. Amen.

PROPHETIC ACT

Declare this over your life: "With God's help, I am tending the garden of my heart. Lies I have believed are being removed, and biblical truth is being planted."

EXTRA RESOURSES

CD: Vallotton, Kris. "Fear Is Not Your Friend," Kris Vallotton Ministries. Available at www.ibethel.org/store.

Book: Bevere, John. *Breaking Intimidation: How to Overcome Fear and Release the Gifts of God in Your Life.* Lake Mary: Strang Communications Company, 1995.

Chapter 5

BOUND IN SPIRIT

"I am bound in spirit to something greater than myself."

CHART OF ENEMY SCHEMES

Below you will find the Chart of Enemy Schemes from chapter 1. We will now look into the enemy scheme of Sabotage.

Enemy Schemes	Sounds Like...	Feels Like...	Remedy
Toil (Evil One) Ex: Cain, Martha Ref: 1 John 3:12	Too busy Too tired Too hard	Inconvenience Drudgery Discouragement Impatience	Sabbath
Fear (Punishment) Ex: Saul (1 Sam. 15:24) Ref: 1 John 4:18	I am afraid I will fail It will hurt I am insecure	Double-mindedness Insecurity/Suspicion Lack of control Insignificance Slavery/Fear of man	Adoption Rom. 8:15
Sabotage (Betrayal) Ex: Joseph Ref: Gen. 50:20	Threats Warnings Abandonment	Trauma Victimization Hopelessness	Courage Vision

Sabotage is the third scheme of the enemy to destroy dreams and the redeemed imagination. Sabotage is different from toil and fear in the orientation of the attack. Toil and fear both work from the inside out, meaning the only demonic power operating in them is that of suggestion. And our only risk is the power of agreement.

Sabotage, on the other hand, operates from the outside in, meaning the enemy attack is external and active upon our assets, purposes, and promises. Examples of sabotage are slanders, legal threats, and physical attacks that externally attack our dreams.

It is important to understand that a poverty spirit will confuse toil and fear with sabotage. This happens because the poverty mentality (beggarly attitude) has become so familiar to us that we believe we are powerless. The poverty mentality will automatically find agreement with the enemy's suggestions.

This is the work of a familiar spirit—we become so familiar with a lie that we believe it originates within ourselves and that it is valid. However, as new creations in Christ, we can overcome internal lies by the law of displacement, planting seeds of biblical truth where lies formerly grew.

Sabotage represents the category of outside attack. Obvious and undeniable, outside attacks seek to steal, kill, and destroy our lives. A poverty mentality that suffers an external attack will personalize these attacks and move into either toil or fear. A Prosperous Soul will overcome these attacks and ultimately see the attacks turn for good in much the same way Joseph saw the plans of his brothers and Potiphar's wife turn for good.

> But Joseph said to them, "Do not be afraid, for am I in God's place? As for you, you meant evil against me, but God meant it for good in order to bring about this present result, to preserve many people alive."
>
> Genesis 50:19-20

> And we know that God causes all things to work together for good to those who love God, to those who are called according to His purpose.
>
> Romans 8:28

THE CALLING OF THE PROSPEROUS SOUL

Believers avoid power and success for many reasons. Some hide in an effort to protect themselves from the enemy. This is called fear. Others are offended by past abuses of power, both inside and outside the church. They feel justified by avoiding money or power. This is also fear. Though hiding serves to protect the individual from the risks that come with influence, it also creates a vacuum of God's people in powerful places. Those who have a worldly perspective control not all, but certainly most, seats of power. We are called to occupy the places of leadership around us, but with those places of leadership come the challenges of affluence.

Up to this point, we have focused on displacing our flawed foundations and belief structures with truth because *money is power, and power exaggerates whatever is in our hearts*. The previous chapters are essential in order to carry the great weight of wealth.

Bethel Church focuses prayer on seven mountains of influence in society. We have defined them as:

Family

Church

Media

Science and Technology

Art and Entertainment

Business

Government

To take this world for the kingdom, God's servants need to occupy positions on every one of these seven mountains. Power flows from the top and sides. But to get to the top, we need to be trained and spiritually prepared in our hearts to handle the power we are given. As we gain access to these places of influence, the pressure at the top of the mountains exaggerates what is in our hearts. Make a list from your own experience of the challenges faced by the leadership at the top of mountains. Pray for the believers who will take those places. Consider this a beginning list of the things God must work out in your own heart in order to entrust you with more.

List five people with positions of leadership around you that are not related to church. These may be senators, mayors, supervisors, and business executives. Place a mark by the ones who are overtly followers of Christ. Take a moment to pray for those who occupy places of power and thank God for their courage. For those positions that are missing godly representation, pray for the vacuum to be filled according to Jesus' will. Consider filling one of those positions yourself.

CALLED TO BE HEROES

As believers, we carry many talents and skills that qualify us to take these places of influence. But I believe the primary characteristic for success on the mountains is courage. Scripture repeatedly encourages us to "have courage."

> But you, be strong and do not lose courage, for there is reward for your work.
>
> 2 Chronicles 15:7

> And they brought to Him a paralytic lying on a bed. Seeing their faith, Jesus said to the paralytic, "Take courage, son; your sins are forgiven."
>
> Matthew 9:2

> Therefore, keep up your courage, men, for I believe God that it will turn out exactly as I have been told.
>
> Acts 27:25

You can always associate the virtue of courage with a Prosperous Soul. Yes, a Prosperous Soul is a content soul, a soul who knows how to enjoy good things, who can take rest and be at leisure and who can sit dreaming as if they had all the time in the world. But the Prosperous Soul doesn't stay seated. Remember the second rule of success from the first chapter? A Prosperous Soul knows how to wield the "long arm of reality" to reach for those dreams with wisdom, strength, and determination. A Prosperous Soul is courageous.

Take a moment to list ten challenges you face in life that require courage.

Based on the previous list, choose three you feel are godly priorities and write them below. Ask God to tutor you on inspired steps and goals to garner courage and overcome these challenges.

BOUND IN SPIRIT

Consider the heroic statement of the apostle Paul:

> And see, now I go bound in the spirit to Jerusalem, not knowing the things that will happen to me there, except that the Holy Spirit testifies in every city, saying that chains and tribulations await me. But none of these things move me; nor do I count my life dear to myself, so that I may finish my race with joy, and the ministry which I received from the Lord Jesus, to testify to the gospel of the grace of God.
>
> Acts 20:22-24 (NKJV)

If the Holy Spirit warned you or me of chains and tribulations lying ahead, how many of us would take such warnings as signs to stay away from those dangers? And yet Paul boldly states that the knowledge that he will suffer does not move him. The only thing that moves him is finishing his race with joy. This is his purpose, and to this purpose, he is *"bound in the spirit."* Here we find the key to courage. A hero's courage is always the result of a spirit bound to a cause greater than oneself.

Pay attention to Paul's phrase *bound in spirit*. The word translated "bound" in the passage above is *deo*, which *Strong's Concordance* tells us is also translated as "bind," "imprisoned," "chained," or "tied."

I've used the term *bondage* to describe the effects of the poverty spirit. But what we see in Paul's testimony is that not all bonds are negative. In fact, fulfilling our purpose as heroes depends upon our being bound to, and bound by, certain things.

We have to be so bound in the truth of the Word and our relationship with the Lord that nothing can shake us at the top of the mountains.

Take a moment and list five things that would be biblically proper to be bound to. One example may be to be bound to God's Word. Another example may be to be bound to your spouse. Review your list and ask God for courage to steward these well.

TOKEN 7: RUBBER BAND

Prophetically, the rubber band symbolizes:

> The flexible nature of being bound in spirit to something

> The necessity of being held to something bigger than yourself

> Courage to persevere in the face of enemy schemes

Stretch the rubber band between your hands. Place it around your right wrist as a prophetic act of being bound to His purposes. Pray the following prayer:

> Father God, I ask You to bind me to Your purposes. Like Paul was bound in spirit for Jerusalem in Acts 20:22, I pray for my courage to rise. Protect me from every enemy scheme, and fan my courage to persevere in the face of any attack that may come. Grant me the favor of Joseph because I believe all things work together for good for those who love You and are called according to Your purpose. Enable me to become a supernatural steward, to glorify You by magnifying You in my heart. I pray this in Jesus' name. Amen.

CREDENTIALS OF THE SUPERNATURAL STEWARD

Imagine the ramifications of the phrase "supernatural steward." What comes to mind when you say it aloud and ponder its potential? List your ideas here.

In addition to courage, a supernatural steward carries these inspired credentials:

A carrier of courage who perseveres in all things

> A recognized servant and "mystery bearer"
>
> A dreamer and redeemed imaginer
>
> A builder of generational legacy
>
> A curious and consistent seeker of wisdom
>
> A person of purpose and intention
>
> A generous giver
>
> A protector and builder of wealth

RECOGNIZED SERVANT AND MYSTERY BEARER

Stewards are those who manage or handle things owned by another. God tells us that we will handle the things owned (everything on earth) and that we will be known because of our servanthood to Christ. Further, we will handle the intangible mysteries of God—He will share with us His secrets. These were the credentials necessary to Joseph's interpretation of Pharaoh's dream. Without the supernatural, we are relegated to ordinary human skill, training, and efficiency. Imagine what God implies here when we are identified as supernatural:

> So then, men ought to regard us as servants of Christ and as those entrusted with the secret things of God.
>
> 1 Corinthians 4:1

DREAMER AND REDEEMED "IMAGINER"

Bill Johnson says that a yielded imagination becomes a sanctified imagination, and a sanctified imagination becomes an invitation for the supernatural to invade. Just harnessing the imagination to picture what the Bible says to be true is safe and extreme.

Made in God's image, saved by Christ's sacrifice, we are uniquely qualified to exercise our redeemed imaginations. This enables us to imitate God. Our success is a glory to our Maker as imitation is the highest form of worship.

BUILDER OF GENERATIONAL LEGACY

Life continually throws unexpected things at us because it is not linear. By that, I mean that economies and governments cycle. Supernatural stewards know this and plan accordingly. Thinking long term, they understand their responsibility of leaving an inheritance. Planning for generations to come is part of our inheritance as believers. Tragically, King Hezekiah began as a successful king of Judah but ultimately failed in the end to protect his legacy by leaving his children to deal with his sins (see Isaiah 39).

> You shall live in the land of Goshen, and you shall be near me, you and your children and your children's children and your flocks and your herds and all that you have.
>
> Genesis 45:10

> When you become the father of children and children's children and have remained long in the land, and act corruptly, and make an idol in the form of anything, and do that which is evil in the sight of the Lord your God so as to provoke Him to anger...
>
> Deuteronomy 4:25

> But the loving kindness of the Lord is from everlasting to everlasting on those who fear Him, and His righteousness to children's children.
>
> Psalm 103:17

> Indeed, may you see your children's children. Peace be upon Israel!
>
> Psalm 128:6

A good man leaves an inheritance to his children's children, and the wealth of the sinner is stored up for the righteous.

Proverbs 13:22

CURIOUS AND CONSISTENT SEEKER OF WISDOM

As you gaze at the mountains of influence, realize you will need knowledge and understanding. Whether you pursue higher education or nurture an ongoing appetite for learning, you will prosper by developing habits of curiosity.

Study your local newspaper or read online national news. Developing a healthy interest in politics is essential for supernatural stewards.

Read books and write about them. I have a robust reading system where I rotate between financial books, biographies, poetry, recreational novels, and classics. Keep exposing yourself to greater minds than yours and sharpen your thinking skills.

PERSON OF PURPOSE AND INTENTION

Supernatural stewards are always moving with intention toward their purposes. They are not given to reckless spending or retail therapy (buying things to make themselves feel better) because they are in control of themselves.

Control is not evil. The difference between a destructive flood and a clean river is control. Without control (focus, boundaries, and order), one cannot expect to build or create anything short of chaos. Even spontaneity and creativity require control. Developing your capacity to carry on intentionally will result in consistency and success as a lifestyle.

In an oversimplified form, all spending can be grouped into three categories:

> Living

> Giving

> Saving

When I counsel individuals and companies on spending plans, I demonstrate how all financial activities should touch each category. Living is the category of operations. These are all the expenses needed to run your life or business. Giving is tithe and offerings—the outflow of your economic engine. Every activity should create strength and benefit those around you. Saving is the amount placed aside for the future. This is the storehouse, and the Bible explains that the storehouse receives a commanded blessing. If you want God's commanded blessings, then you need to give Him a target to bless—which is your savings (see Deuteronomy 28:8).

GENEROUS GIVER

Each expenditure should be strategic. Living expenses should be controlled and never wasted. Spend only on purpose, not haphazardly or accidentally (see Proverbs 27:23). Even giving is strategic.

Some Christians are called by God to live the life of an ascetic (the practice of strict self-discipline and abstention from indulgence). Others are led by God to give everything away to the poor and financially begin again. Both of these extremes are rare events and not for every Christian. I respect and celebrate those who have taken these roads but caution other believers. I have heard it said, "We can't out give God." I agree in theory but suggest that, short of the rare callings of ascetics, most believers are called to give to the poor, and you cannot do that when you have nothing. Orphans and widows need to be cared for and we are called to honor kings with our treasuries (tithing and honoraria). We can't do these things when we are homeless and destitute. We are here to finance His kingdom on earth. Missions take money and I believe we can out give God when we irresponsibly waste our seed on rocky soil, eat all of our seed, or sow our bread. Living beyond your means will create an economic hole that can weaken or cripple your purpose in God.

> Now such persons we command and exhort in the Lord Jesus Christ to work in quiet fashion and eat their own bread.
>
> 2 Thessalonians 3:12

I believe the principle of sowing and reaping implies an understanding of seed and bread. Seed represents what we sow, or give away, and results in increase—some thirty, sixty, and a hundredfold.

Bread represents what we eat. This is your personal economic engine designed to accomplish the purpose you have in Christ. Be aware that guilt and manipulation could emotionally motivate your feelings to give everything away, to the point of destroying your economic engines.

This is a mystery of God—one that supernatural stewards will manage. They will understand when to give radically and cheerfully and when to withhold for the purposes God has set before them.

PROTECTOR AND BUILDER OF WEALTH

Living within your means will create a powerful economic engine for good in the hands of a Prosperous Soul. Spending less than you earn will guarantee the creation of net worth. The Prosperous Soul uses wealth to create a shock absorber around themselves and others. For example, Joseph's answer to Pharaoh was a national tax to create a storehouse. The plan was an effective bumper to absorb the devastation of a seven-year famine.

> As for you, you meant evil against me, but God meant it for good in order to bring about this present result, to preserve many people alive.
>
> Genesis 50:20

Consider that money, riches, and wealth are for a greater purpose than your personal comfort and pleasure. Accumulated riches become a powerful force for good when managed by inspired men and women. Like Joseph, I believe we are to build a storehouse for times of trouble. A storehouse is an inventory of time. For example, workers sell their time and earn a wage. Working by the hour, they receive their pay and place a residual part into savings. They are literally storing time.

> This is a helpful perspective because wealth is not measured by unit and value but in time. Net worth is a measure of how much time is in inventory. To help clarify this concept, ask yourself these questions: "How much time do I have in savings if my income stream stopped today? Would I last a week on my savings? A month? A year?"

Your answers to those questions will tell you how much time you have inventoried. The supernatural steward creates a storehouse. They manage an inventory of time.

Consider some ways to create a bumper of time around you. Most see this as an emergency fund. What are some steps you can take to begin to build a storehouse around your life?

Additionally, a supernatural steward understands and works toward multiple streams of income. They combine the power of earned income (wages) with passive income. Passive income includes interest, dividends, royalties, and rents. These streams of income continue even when you stop working. They are the best examples of having money work for you rather than you working for money.

Finally, the supernatural steward understands how to protect the wealth that has been created. Many middle-class Americans know how to work hard and create streams of income. The difference between the average person and the sophisticated investor is the knowledge of protection. The moment of wealth lies at the heart of economic transfers. Wealth is seldom lost; rather, it is moved or transferred between those who made it and those who know how to contain it. When housing prices are rising, the average person is buying assets, whereas the sophisticated investor is selling properties purchased years earlier when prices were falling. They may have paid a fraction of the value then and now are netting a large gain when they sell it in a rising market (see Proverbs 31). The headline financial news that the average person reads is already dated; the economic train left the station way before the news was public knowledge.

This cycle of rising and falling is overcome by the supernatural steward, one who learns to rise and hold, rise and hold. Wealth accumulates and grows rather than suffering loss and having to begin again. This is the transfer of wealth happening every day in large and small ways across the world of economics. It was the very principle Joseph used when he converted grain (which had become virtually worthless in the first seven years) into gold for Pharaoh.

Review these credentials of the supernatural steward:

A carrier of courage who perseveres in all things

A recognized servant and "mystery bearer"

A dreamer and redeemed imaginer

A builder of generational legacy

A curious and consistent seeker of wisdom

A person of purpose and intention

A generous giver

A protector and builder of wealth

Write each of these on a sheet of paper and prayerfully ask God to reveal how you can develop them in your life. Write down what the Holy Spirit tells you. I strongly encourage you to check out the extra resources in the lesson overview.

LESSONS
Chapter 5

HOMEWORK

In two or three paragraphs, describe your perfect day. This exercise uses your redeemed imagination to tell how you would spend your time, from dawn to dusk, living your perfect day. File this somewhere you can access it from time to time.

VIDEO

Watch "Bound in Spirit (Parts I, II, and III)" on your DVD or in the online curriculum.

GOING DEEPER

What does it mean to be "bound in spirit"?

How can you become a steward of the mysteries of God?

Do you feel you're called to any of the mountains of influence? If so, how can you move forward to step into this calling?

How does seeing yourself as a powerful person affect the dream list you started in chapter 1?

If your money ran out today, how much "time" do you have saved in your storehouses?

Spend 10 minutes in prayer seeking God's heart for your finances. Then answer these questions: What did He show you? How does this revelation help you set goals for the future and move forward with purpose?

Does living within your means sound achievable to you? If not, what are some things you can cut back on to make sure you live with intention and focus?

FURTHER STUDY

Read *Money and the Prosperous Soul* (chapter 6).

Read or memorize Acts 20:22–24 (NKJV).

Explore the subjects of legacy, bound in spirit, and commanded blessing in the Bible.

Review Token 7 (rubber band).

PRAYER

Father God, I ask You to bind me to Your purposes. Protect me from every enemy scheme that may come as I work to fulfill my calling on this earth. Enable me to become a supernatural steward—one who glorifies You in all seasons of life. I pray this all in Jesus' name. Amen.

PROPHETIC ACT

Declare over yourself, "I am bound in spirit to something greater than myself."

EXTRA RESOURSES

For more information on Lance Wallnau Ministries, his books and sermons, Seven Mountains, or 7M School, go to www.lancelearning.com.

Book: Jandl, Al, and Van Crouch. *The Storehouse Principle: A Revolutionary God Idea for Creating Extraordinary Financial Stability.* Broken Arrow: CrossStaff Publishers, LLC, 2004.

Book: Morris, Robert. *The Blessed Life*. Ventura: Regal Books, 2004. (Originally published by Gateway Church, 2002.)

Book: Stanley, Thomas J. *The Millionaire Mind*. Kansas City, MO: Andrew McMeel Publishing, LLC, 2001.

Chapter 6

SPIRIT OF MAMMON

---

*"I am not mastered by money, riches, or wealth.
They serve God through my hands."*

SPIRIT OF MAMMON

Inevitably, the Prosperous Soul will abound in blessing. This believer will supernaturally prosper and enjoy divine health as an outgrowth of prosperity of soul. As we are faithful in little and God presents us with much, we will find ourselves sailing into new waters. Our course will lead us away from the influence of the poverty spirit forever. However, a new hazard, one God specifically warns of and requires to be mastered, often appears on the horizon—the spirit of Mammon.

> No one can serve two masters; for either he will hate the one and love the other, or he will be devoted to one and despise the other. You cannot serve God and wealth.
>
> Matthew 6:24

It can be uncomfortable to use words such as *power, success,* and *influence* within the Christian world, but that is exactly where Christ has called us. Yet in that success, we cannot serve two masters.

What is a biblical definition of success? To speak concisely, I believe success can be biblically defined as displaying God's kingdom on earth, as it is in heaven. Let's look again at the rules of success we studied in chapter 1:

If you can't dream it, you can't have it.

Reach out with the long arm of reality.

Timing

Now I would like to add a fourth rule, taken from Viktor Frankl's book *Man's Search for Meaning:*

Don't aim at success. It must ensue.

Viktor Frankl was victimized by the worst of humanity—the concentration camps of Nazi Germany during the 1930s. There he observed the nature of suffering and human struggle. I find it interesting that he penned this observation on success in such a context:

Don't aim at success—the more you aim at it and make it a target, the more you are going to miss it. For success, like happiness, cannot be pursued; it must ensue, and it only does so as the unintended side effect of one's personal dedication to a cause greater than oneself or as the by-product of one's surrender to a person other than oneself. Happiness must happen, and the same holds for success—you have to let it happen by not caring about it[5].

In this, I find the final wrap on a Prosperous Soul. You must be. A Prosperous Soul is not one that is behaved but one that is lived. It is a life lived for God in both public and private. It is a life lived from authenticity. From this, we safely position ourselves for breakthrough and protect ourselves from breaking upon the shores of Mammon. The Prosperous Soul defines success not from objectives but from the heart.

ABOUT MAMMON

Different versions of Scripture translate the word *Mammon* in unique ways.

The New International Version uses *riches.*

The New American Standard Bible chose *wealth.*

Others prefer the word *money.*

Unfortunately, each of these translations was an attempt to capture a word that is unfamiliar to our Western minds. Mammon is much different from simply riches, money, or wealth. The actual word is the greek word, *Mammonas.* Its original source is Chaldee (Babylonian) and means:

To place your confidence in, or personify, wealth

To deify wealth, or to worship or treat riches as a god

Mammon is a mastering spirit. It operates in opposition to the kingdom because it is a ruler. Jesus warns us to beware of the mastering characteristic of Mammon—a spirit that causes us to see differently. Consequently, Jesus declares an absolute prohibition against this spirit, saying we can't serve God and Mammon (see Matthew 6:24).

---

5   Viktor E. Frankl, *Man's Search for Meaning* (New York: Pocket Books, 1959).

I find these aspects of Mammon sobering:

> Mammon is not money, riches, or wealth but "wealth personified" or "riches deified."

> Mammon is a proper name since it is a "person."

> Mammon is a mastering spirit, one that displaces God in our sight.

> Mammon completely embezzles anything we steward.

> God hates Mammon and Mammon hates God.

> Mammon is our destroyer.

Our mandatory goal as Prosperous Souls is to master, and not be mastered by, Mammon. This is a directive given by Jesus Himself in a curious passage in Luke 16, beginning with verse 1 (emphasis mine):

> Now He was also saying to the disciples, "There was a rich man who had a manager, and this manager was reported to him as squandering his possessions."

Where the NASB translators use the word *manager*, read *steward*. I believe the steward in this passage had succumbed to the spirit of Mammon, being mastered by it rather than mastering it. He had become a lover of money or a worshiper of this deity called Mammonas.

> And he called him and said to him, "What is this I hear about you? Give an accounting of your management, for you can no longer be manager."

> Luke 16:2

Verse 2 clearly indicates the disqualification of the steward's fitness to continue working for the rich man. This point is sometimes forgotten later (verse 8) when the rich man praises the dishonest steward for his shrewdness. More on that later; let's press on through verses 3–7:

> The manager said to himself, "What shall I do, since my master is taking the management away from me? I am not strong to dig; I am ashamed to beg. I know what I shall do, so that when I am removed from the management people will welcome me into their homes." And he summoned each one of his master's debtors, and he began saying to the first, "How much do you owe my master?" And he said, "A hundred measures of oil." And he said to him, "Take your bill, and sit down quickly and write fifty." Then he said to another, "And how much do you owe?" And he said, "A hundred measures of wheat." He said to him, "Take your bill, and write eighty."

> Luke 16:3-7

The steward faces the destructive result of worshiping Mammon. His position is lost, his career ruined, and he faces begging as a means of fending off starvation. In this condition, his sight returns; money, riches, and wealth are to be mastered, not to be mastered by. He quickly shifts gears, forsaking *the love of money*, and begins to make deals in the few relationships that remain. This information gets back to the master, who has an interesting response to the steward's thievery.

> And his master praised the unrighteous manager because he had acted shrewdly; for the sons of this age are more shrewd in relation to their own kind than the sons of light.

> Luke 16:8

The master praises the steward on his shrewdness, but don't be confused. Remember that the steward was not reinstated. He was still disqualified and faced a destroyed career and the strong possibility of begging for his survival.

What the master praised, however, was the abandonment of the worship of Mammon. Money became a tool again, not a deity. Though it was too late for the steward's career with the master, perhaps it was a lesson learned well for his future. Jesus leaves the parable and speaks directly to His disciples in verse 9:

> And I say to you, make friends for yourselves by means of the wealth of unrighteousness, so that when it fails they will receive you into the eternal dwellings.
>
> Luke 16:9

Jesus strikes hard on the lesson for stewards. Money is a tool to be mastered, not to be mastered by. In itself, it will fail because money, riches, and possessions are not the currencies, treasures, or assets of heaven. They are merely tools to be used here in this brief time we have on earth. Their purpose is to be used; with them we show ourselves faithful in little so that we may be found faithful to steward the true riches mentioned in verse 11:

> He who is faithful in a very little thing is faithful also in much; and he who is unrighteous in a very little thing is unrighteous also in much.
>
> Luke 16:10

Here, Jesus lays out the foundational truths of supernatural stewardship and the occupation of a Prosperous Soul. In verses 11 and 12, He goes on to explain that unrighteous Mammon has its purpose—to be mastered. As Christians, we are not to hide from wealth and power because our function is one of discerning faithfulness. This brings us back to chapter 5: being bound in our spirits to Christ's purpose.

> Therefore if you have not been faithful in the use of unrighteous wealth, who will entrust the true riches to you? And if you have not been faithful in the use of that which is another's, who will give you that which is your own?
>
> Luke 16:11–12

Jesus summarizes the point of His parable in verse 13. Mammon is a mastering spirit; unrighteous Mammon is wealth personified.

> "No servant can serve two masters; for either he will hate the one and love the other, or else he will be devoted to one and despise the other. You cannot serve God and wealth." Now the Pharisees, who were lovers of money, were listening to all these things and were scoffing at Him.
>
> Luke 16:13-14

FINGERPRINTS OF MAMMON

Studying Mammon reveals a tension—we must learn to master unrighteous Mammon, while recognizing that the very thing we handle seeks to master us. I learned that a Mammon spirit leaves these clues like fingerprints:

Mammon thrives on secrecy and untruth.

Mammon encourages unhealthy comparisons and factions between individuals and groups.

Mammon hungers for immoral and sensuous living.

Mammon is an incubator for most addictions.

Mammon promotes greed and envy of others' success.

COMPARISON OF MAMMON AND POVERTY

The effects of Mammon are distinctly different from those of the poverty spirit.

SPIRIT OF MAMMON	SPIRIT OF POVERTY
Promotes you	Hides you
Tells you to strive (toil)	Tells you to give up
Pushes you forward	Holds you back
Calls you lord (Luke 12:18)	Calls you worthless
Self-promotion	Self-condemnation
Boastful pride of life	Victim mentality
Factions between "us" and "them"	Fights to hold others down
Materialism	Impulse buying (consumerism)
Envy	Jealousy
Lusts for possessions (people, luxuries)	Hordes junk
Affluence and social climbing	Obscurity and invisibility
Sensuous living	Money flees from you
Lying and secrecy	Complaining and bitterness
Slavery to addictions	Slavery to lack
Trusts in fame (not God)	Trusts in self (not God)
Lives in bondage (indebtedness)	Never enough
Businesses subjugate people (Revelation 18:13)	Businesses struggle and fail

DEFEATING THE SPIRIT OF MAMMON

You cannot serve God and Mammon, but you can serve God with wealth when you are bound in spirit to God's agenda. Realize that a fear of riches isn't based on the riches themselves but on what binds your heart. If your heart is pure, wealth becomes useful. God sees your faithfulness with money.

Defeating the spirit of Mammon is easy when our hearts are bound to Christ's purposes. Mammon is broken by the Macedonian grace Paul spoke of to the Corinthian church. A brief study of historical Macedonia reveals a region torn by warfare and hardship. Yet Paul celebrates their generosity and encourages the Corinthian church to adopt their forceful and intentional generosity.

> Now, brethren, we wish to make known to you the grace of God which has been given in the churches of Macedonia, that in a great ordeal of affliction their abundance of joy and their deep poverty overflowed in the wealth of their liberality. For I testify that according to their ability, and beyond their ability, they gave of their own accord, begging us with much urging for the favor of participation in the support of the saints, and this, not as we had expected, but they first gave themselves to the Lord and to us by the will of God.
>
> 2 Corinthians 8:1–5

This kind of giving is nothing less than spiritual violence against strongholds of Mammon (and poverty as well). Paul goes on in the next chapter and coins the phrase "cheerful giver":

> Now this I say, he who sows sparingly will also reap sparingly, and he who sows bountifully will also reap bountifully. Each one must do just as he has purposed in his heart, not grudgingly or under compulsion, for God loves a cheerful giver. And God is able to make all grace abound to you, so that always having all sufficiency in everything, you may have an abundance for every good deed.
>
> 2 Corinthians 9:6–7

Radical generosity, to the point of sacrifice, is the primary weapon against Mammon. Cheerful givers understand what they are giving away; they know what they are sacrificing, and they do it anyway. This is the grace to give with understanding.

TOKEN 8: ALUMINUM FOIL

Prophetically, the aluminum foil symbolizes:

> The shiny appeal of Mammon

> The ability of Mammon to wrap around anything if we are not careful and aware

> The inherent usefulness of unrighteous Mammon

Taking the foil in your hand, roll it into a ball. Consider how Mammon is appealing, adaptable, and useful in the right hand of a supernatural steward, but it is disastrous and idolatrous to those who permit themselves to be mastered by it. Pray this prayer aloud and write down any revelations you hear from the Holy Spirit as a result.

> Father God, I will not keep my finances a secret. I will not keep hidden the issues You reveal. I will be open before You, King, and allow Your Holy Spirit to guide and direct me, to heal and reveal and destroy any influence of the spirit of Mammon in my life. Teach me, God, not to be used. For money is a good slave but a terrible master. You are my One true God and the lover of my soul. I plan to keep it that way with Your help. I pray this in Jesus' name. Amen.

Place your hand on your heart and make the following declaration over your spirit: "I am a Prosperous Soul free of the spirit of Mammon, bound in spirit to Christ, and able to serve a faithful God."

LESSONS
Chapter 6

HOMEWORK

Practice being the master of your money. Carry a single $100 bill in your wallet for one full month without spending it. During this time, ask God to show you, at the proper time, how to sow the $100. If you are provoked to give before the month is ended, use other dollars; consider this bill your prisoner and do not allow it to "escape" for any reason. At the end of the month, sow it in a place the Lord directs you. Journal how this makes you feel.

VIDEO

Watch "Spirit of Mammon (Parts I and II)" on your DVD or in the online curriculum.

GOING DEEPER

Describe Mammon in your own words.

How does seeing Mammon as "wealth deified" rather than wealth itself change your perspective on money?

Are any of Mammon's "fingerprints" present in your life?

What are some steps you can take to "tune out" Mammon's broadcasts?

How does Mammon push you out ahead of God's timing?

What is God's heart for money? How can you master it to bring healing to the nations?

FURTHER STUDY

Read *Money and the Prosperous Soul* (chapter 7).

Read or memorize Luke 16:10–14.

Explore the subjects of greed, Macedonian grace, cheerful giver, and Mammon in the Bible.

Review Token 8 (aluminum foil).

PRAYER

Father God, I will not keep my finances a secret. I will be open before You and allow Your Holy Spirit to guide and direct me—to heal and reveal and destroy any influence of the spirit of Mammon in my life. Teach me, God, not to be used. For money is a good slave but a terrible master. You are my One true God and the lover of my soul. I plan to keep it that way with Your help. I pray this in Jesus' name. Amen.

PROPHETIC ACT

Declare: "I am not mastered by money, riches, or wealth. They serve God through my hands."

EXTRA RESOURSES

Read a local or national newspaper's financial section eight times in a 30-day period. Write down the themes you discover.

Develop a personal debt relief plan and stick to it for one year.

Take a basic investing class at your local community college.

Book: Alcorn, Randy. *Money, Possessions and Eternity.* Eternal Perspective Ministries by Tyndale House Publishers, Inc., 2003.

Book: Frankl, Viktor. *Man's Search for Meaning.* New York: Pocket Books, 1984.

Book: Wuthnow, Robert. *God and Mammon in America.* New York: A Division of Macmillan, Inc., 2003.

Chapter 7

DOMINION

---

*"I am in dominion, under heaven's authority,
and a co-heir with Christ."*

THE TREE OF LIFE

Man was created in God's image and placed in an environment of perfect authority. God was the head, and Adam and Eve were authorized to rule over all the earth. They were designed for dominion.

> God created man in His own image, in the image of God He created him; male and female He created them. God blessed them; and God said to them, "Be fruitful and multiply, and fill the earth, and subdue it; and rule over the fish of the sea and over the birds of the sky and over every living thing that moves on the earth." Then God said, "Behold, I have given you every plant yielding seed that is on the surface of all the earth, and every tree which has fruit yielding seed; it shall be food for you; and to every beast of the earth and to every bird of the sky and to every thing that moves on the earth which has life, I have given every green plant for food"; and it was so. God saw all that He had made, and behold, it was very good. And there was evening and there was morning, the sixth day.
>
> Genesis 1:27–31

And in that creation, the tree of life was planted from the beginning of the world. In Genesis it was a desirable tree, one perhaps that provided eternal life to the partaker. It seems God had always intended for man to live forever and to reign. But that plan was changed by man's failure with sin. Therefore, God assigned an angel to barricade access to the tree until a Savior dealt with man's sin, lest man be lost into eternal life in sin.

> So He drove the man out; and at the east of the garden of Eden He stationed the cherubim and the flaming sword which turned every direction to guard the way to the tree of life.
>
> Genesis 3:24

Jesus Christ came as the perfect Man to repay the debt of sin. For those who believe this and confess Jesus as Lord and Savior, God removes the stain of their sin forever, leaving them once again justified and blameless after their failures and mistakes.

> But what does it say? "The word is near you, in your mouth and in your heart"—that is, the word of faith which we are preaching, that if you confess with your mouth Jesus as Lord, and believe in your heart that God raised Him from the dead, you will be saved; for with the heart a person believes, resulting in righteousness, and with the mouth he confesses, resulting in salvation. For the Scripture says, "Whoever believes in Him will not be disappointed." For there is no distinction between Jew and Greek; for the same Lord is Lord of all, abounding in riches for all who call on Him; for "Whoever will call on the name of the Lord will be saved."
>
> Romans 10:8–13

We see the tree of life appear again in Revelation 22; only this time, it is planted in the New Jerusalem, which is the kingdom reestablished by God at the end of time. Imagine this beautiful scene as you read John's account slowly. Remember, he is describing for us something that he actually saw with an angelic tour guide.

> Then he showed me a river of the water of life, clear as crystal, coming from the throne of God and of the Lamb, in the middle of its street. On either side of the river was the tree of life, bearing twelve kinds of fruit, yielding its fruit every month; and the leaves of the tree were for the healing of the nations.
>
> Revelations 22:1–2

Again, we are isolated from the tree of life until this future time when we walk in heaven. Yet Jesus explained earlier to this same John that He came to provide abundant life (see John 10:10). And Paul declares that God is able to do far more abundantly beyond all we ask or think (see Ephesians 3:20). I believe the tree of life is still accessible, here, between Genesis and Revelation, where we are living out our daily lives. Christ is the key, and Solomon tells us how to turn the key.

Hope deferred makes the heart sick, but desire fulfilled is a tree of life.

Proverbs 13:12 (emphasis mine)

I believe that a Prosperous Soul has deeply embraced the truth that Jesus is the Christ and the desire of all nations and peoples. Haggai 2:7 prophesies that the world will come with the wealth of all nations, and God will fill His house with glory. The word *wealth* is better translated "desire" or "delight." Read the Haggai verse now as the declaration it was intended to be:

"I will shake all the nations; and they will come with the [desire] of all nations, and I will fill this house with glory," says the Lord of hosts.

Haggai 2:7

I believe this is a global salvation. The tree of life is available for everyone because desire fulfilled in Jesus Christ is a tree of life. Today, every believer in Jesus can "return to the garden" and experience the dominion in which God designed us to walk.

Dominion, by definition, brings together two dimensions: authority and ownership. Understanding dominion thus depends upon understanding how these two elements function together.

AUTHORITY

The fundamental principle of authority is that it can only be given to you. And when someone gives you authority, it is always related to a specific task or set of tasks. *Exousia,* the Greek word translated "authority," can also be translated "power" or "right." Consider what the apostle John said about the *exousia* of the believer:

> But as many as received Him, to them He gave the right [exousia] to become children of God, even to those who believe in His name.
>
> John 1:12

Walking as children of God is the defining, fundamental "task" we have been divinely authorized to perform. This means leaving behind poverty and all that we learned as spiritual orphans and learning to imitate Christ, the model of a mature child of God. Doing these things is not simply a good idea; it is imperative. Then, as mature children, we are authorized to teach others:

> All authority has been given to Me in heaven and on earth. Go therefore and make disciples of all the nations, baptizing them in the name of the Father and the Son and the Holy Spirit, teaching them to observe all that I commanded you; and lo, I am with you always, even to the end of the age.
>
> Matthew 28:18

The Great Commission did not come with a ten-step model or a business plan. It came with Christ's promise to be with us always, showing us how to be children of God, just as He is God's Son, and how to invite others into sonship. Our authority to walk in dominion comes from God as we simply follow His lead in everything, just as He followed His Father's lead.

SIGNS OF AUTHORITY

Authority requires credentials. Even Jesus was asked to show His credentials as He baffled the chief priests and elders with supernatural wisdom, miracles, and healings:

> When He entered the temple, the chief priests and the elders of the people came to Him while He was teaching, and said, "By what authority are You doing these things, and who gave You this authority?"
>
> Matthew 21:23

> Rabbi, we know that You have come from God as a teacher; for no one can do these signs that You do unless God is with him.

> John 3:2

Our authority will be displayed by the fruit we bear. Since our behavior always reveals where our trust actually rests, it is normal to show off the King who gives us authority. These displays are known in Scripture as *following signs* (see chapter 1).

> These signs will accompany those who have believed: in My name they will cast out demons, they will speak with new tongues; they will pick up serpents, and if they drink any deadly poison, it will not hurt them; they will lay hands on the sick, and they will recover.

> Mark 16:17–18

For the Prosperous Soul, your following signs will include these and others. Supernatural wisdom will be displayed in your life. Others will seek you out for financial strength and stability. You will understand the times and exercise sound financial decisions. Your generosity will grow and you will help the poor, orphans, and widows. You will display a culture of honor in your words and deeds.

> But just say the word, and my servant will be healed. For I also am a man placed under authority, with soldiers under me; and I say to this one, "Go!" and he goes, and to another, "Come!" and he comes, and to my slave, "Do this!" and he does it.

> Luke 7:7–8

OWNERSHIP

The other element of dominion is *ownership*. This is the demonstration of spiritual maturity as we move from hirelings to sons or daughters. This is where we move from receivers to generous benefactors who distribute the supernatural abundance of our Father's kingdom. We begin to act as mature co-heirs, no longer held by childish ways.

> Now I say, as long as the heir is a child, he does not differ at all from a slave although he is owner of everything, but he is under guardians and managers until the date set by the father. So also we, while we were children, were held in bondage under elemental things of the world. But when the fullness of the time came, God sent forth His Son, born of a woman, born under the Law, so that He might redeem those who were under the Law, that we might receive the adoption as sons. Because you are sons, God has sent forth the Spirit of His Son into our hearts, crying, "Abba! Father!" Therefore you are no longer a slave, but a son; and if a son, then an heir through God.
>
> Galatians 4:1–7

This is the revelation of ownership. Jesus said that our Father *"has chosen gladly"* to give us the kingdom (see Luke 12:32). This promise seems vague and overwhelming until we see that it means we can't fully manage the family business without having access to its resources. It would be inconceivable for God to authorize Jesus to fulfill His destiny as the Messiah without also giving Him the wealth of the kingdom to back that authority. Likewise, Joseph could hardly oversee his storehouse strategy in Egypt without being able to act as owner of the nation's resources. All authority must be provided with a measure of ownership. And dominion, by definition, requires the ownership of a *kingdom*.

The evidence that we are mature, however, is that we use what we have been given. Take note of this description of Solomon's dominion:

> Solomon's provision for one day was thirty kors of fine flour and sixty kors of meal, ten fat oxen, twenty pasture-fed oxen, a hundred sheep besides deer, gazelles, roebucks, and fattened fowl. For he had dominion over everything west of the River, from Tiphsah even to Gaza, over all the kings west of the River; and he had peace on all sides around about him.
>
> 1 Kings 4:22–24 (emphasis mine)

Solomon's dominion was expressed by his ability to harness the wealth of the land for kingly purposes, and so it is with mature believers who walk in dominion. Paul's ability to access Christ's strength in every kind of situation, Joseph's ability to access divine revelation every time he was presented with a dream, or Jesus' ability to heal all who came to Him are all defining marks of mature sons of God who know how to use their spiritual possessions.

STANDING IN THE CRYSTAL RIVER

Dominion is the mature response of a Prosperous Soul. It requires humility and integrity to carry the powers of money, and a wise person will not jump in hastily. Consider the calling of a Prosperous Soul, of being a Joseph or a Josephine who supernaturally stewards the authority of Christ's kingdom. Ask the Holy Spirit if you are called to maturity, to dominion. Write down your prayer and any correction or direction the Spirit may give you.

When you are ready, read the following passage, allowing your redeemed imagination to see a vision of the tree of life, the crystal river, and the throne of God. The word vision comes from a root word that means to behold, envision, or prophesy. Hebrews 5:14 describes the mature as those *"who because of practice have their senses trained to discern good and evil." Practice training your senses.* Close your eyes. Imagine yourself standing in the crystal river of Revelation 22:

> Then he showed me a river of the water of life, clear as crystal, coming from the throne of God and of the Lamb, in the middle of its street. On either side of the river was the tree of life, bearing twelve kinds of fruit, yielding its fruit every month; and the leaves of the tree were for the healing of the nations. There will no longer be any curse; and the throne of God and of the Lamb will be in it, and His bond-servants will serve Him; they will see His face, and His name will be on their foreheads. And there will no longer be any night; and they will not have need of the light of a lamp nor the light of the sun, because the Lord God will illumine them; and they will reign forever and ever.
>
> Revelation 22:1–5

TOKEN 9: RIVER STONE

Prophetically, the river stone symbolizes:

Your position in the crystal river of time (see Revelation 22)

Spiritual maturity to walk as an owner and co-heir of the kingdom

Authority to demonstrate heaven's credentials (following signs)

Dominion as a Prosperous Soul

Imagine you are facing downstream. God is placing good things into the crystal river for you. Yet you are a spectator, watching good things float past you just out of reach. Wait here with God until this picture begins to seem real to you.

Pay attention to your surroundings. In fact, try to use all five senses. Listen for sounds. Smell the aromas and feel the river swirling around your waist. Look around in the spirit and notice the depth of the water and the banks of the river. The throne of God and the tree of life are behind you, but take your time. You'll turn around soon enough. Tarry here for a moment, and write down what you notice, even if it is subtle.

Still facing downstream, imagine that there are gifts in the river, coming from God's throne. These gifts float downstream and perhaps bump against your back and float past. You reach for these gifts, but they are difficult to capture because you are facing downstream and the current moves them on before you are aware of their presence. Permit yourself to experience the sensation of things moving away from you, out of reach, lost to the river. This is a prophetic exercise of what it is like to face downstream. It is the way most people experience promises and benefits throughout their lifetimes—good things come and are lost or missed. Prosperous Souls have a different experience, so prepare for a shift. Pray this prayer:

> Father God, I am standing in the crystal river of time. This river is flowing from the throne of God and of the Lamb. You are filling the river with good things. Because I am facing downstream, good things flow away from me. They are just beyond my reach, too hard to catch.

Pause until this perspective becomes clear to you. When you can imagine the scene, continue praying aloud:

> Lord Jesus, I want to turn. I want to see Your throne. I want to see Your provision. I turn around in Jesus' name.

Physically turn around to face the opposite direction. Again, pause until you can envision the new perspective. When you can "see" the scene, continue praying aloud:

> I am facing upstream by the grace of God.
> I can see the throne of God and the Lamb.
>
> Good things are coming to me.
> The good things are everywhere, here in the river.
>
> There is more than I can contain.
> There is abundance here for everyone.
> Even for me. I receive Your good gifts in Jesus' name.
>
> Amen.

Write down what you have seen, how you feel, or what you heard during this prophetic exercise.

POSITIONING IN THE RIVER

You have just experienced a powerful prophetic act. You will encounter new thoughts and circumstances now that you face upstream in the river. You will need to develop new habits as you practice facing upstream (see Hebrews 5). Look, listen, smell, taste, and feel. Describe it. Write out your testimony of what God is showing you.

Facing upstream, you can see the tree of life bearing fruit. Revelation 22:2 says that it yields its fruit every month. Imagine a tree that passes through four seasons every thirty days. It would bud and leaf, growing lush until fruit hung ripe. Then the fruit would fall and leaves would follow. Below, the crystal river flows from the throne of God, carrying the fruit and leaves to you every month. Now that you're facing upstream, you can observe the fruit and leaves drifting toward you. You can move about, side to side, in order to obtain the good things coming your way. This is the lesson of positioning.

TOKEN 10: CINNAMON STICK

Prophetically, the cinnamon symbolizes:

Anointing. Cinnamon was an original element of anointing oil (see Exodus 30:22–25).

Preservation. Historically cinnamon was used to preserve meat.

Nourishment. Cinnamon is the only raw spice that is edible.

Intimacy. Cinnamon is a perfumer's ingredient.

Healing. Historically cinnamon was used as a medicine.

Since there is so much available from the river, we still need to learn to be wise stewards and understand what God has for us. No matter what we need, God will provide it. The river exercise is one way to position ourselves to receive His good benefits as Prosperous Souls who stand in dominion (authority and ownership). Consider what you need in the mission God has bound you to. If you need encouragement (nourishment), protection (preservation), power (anointing), intimacy or healing, these are all available to you from God. Envision the river once again as you face upstream. Ask God for eyes to see His good benefits coming and wisdom to know how to position yourself in the river to receive His benefits. Write down what you see and hear.

NEW PRACTICES

Facing upstream will require different behaviors as you begin to think from this new perspective. Understand that your circumstances may not change immediately but your viewpoint has.

You may find that, facing upstream for the first time in your life, you begin to see many benefits coming to you that used to just pass you by. As you develop the ability to recognize these, you are learning a key skill of a Prosperous Soul. Many wealthy individuals cite the ability to recognize opportunities as one of the main differences between themselves and those who never succeed.

Next, with all these good things approaching you, it is tempting to say "yes" too many times. I remember my own turning in the river. As these benefits came within reach, I grabbed everything. Although I was breaking free of the poverty spirit, I still had the habits of hoarding because I still believed these gifts from God would run out. Soon I had too much and I learned that the river was filled with *good, better,* and *best* things. I had to allow what was good to pass by, along with the better. My practice became saying "yes" only to the best—those things that best fit my God-given purpose.

I began making decisions (to say "yes") with intention and not availability. The things I allowed to pass by were left to others in the river below me. And, seeing how there were endless benefits coming to me in the river, I found many chances to pick the best.

Another lesson learned in the river is that we naturally turn downstream. Facing upstream is supernatural. It requires a habit of holiness to turn upstream because the soul, like a natural man in a natural river, will turn downstream rather than face the resistance of the current. It is natural to face downstream, even when the river is spiritual.

Finally, in the river you learn to rest. As the realization soaks into your heart that there really is a continual supply of benefits and opportunities (fruit and leaves) falling into the river and flowing to you, you will slow down and relax. You will experience more peace in God's ability to supply "seed to the sower" than ever before (see 2 Corinthians 9:10).

By the way, my personal experience in the river has resulted in plenty of errors. I've said "yes" when I should have said "no" and vice versa. I have regretted allowing the best to pass when I should have taken it. However, even here, God demonstrates His endless, unlimited, and extravagant goodness. I found that missed opportunities are soon replaced with another best. He proves Himself wildly faithful and gracious.

Facing upstream gives you time to position yourself in the river to capture new and different gifts. In fact, God will lead you to new parts of the river. He loves to lead. He is a Wind and expects us to follow His Spirit. There are no stagnant places in Christ.

> God is spirit, and those who worship Him must worship in spirit and truth.
>
> John 4:24

As you look upstream, pray again and this time make it a prophetic declaration:

Father God, Your best gifts are flowing toward me in an endless river of opportunities and benefits. There is no limitation in heaven. You place in the river anointings, callings and appointments, protection and preservation, encouragement and strength, intimacy, healing and health. Good, better, and best things flow to me. They are easy to take hold of. I do not need to grab everything, because You will show me the best. I will not settle for distractions—I want only Your best. I am at rest, and You are training my senses in the crystal river of Revelation 22. Teach me prosperity and dominion, and make me a Prosperous Soul. I pray these things in Jesus' name. Amen.

Take a moment and write down anything God may speak to you now.

FINAL ACT

Token 11: Nickel

Thank you for persevering to the end of this chapter. I trust you have found this course worthwhile as you exercise your spirit in becoming a Prosperous Soul. This final section is simply my commission, that you will continue to succeed in all that God has imagined for your destiny. My final token is always the nickel, which holds a very special message for me. All U.S. coins are named for their value or denomination. There is only one U.S. coin named for what it is made from—the nickel.

Prophetically, the nickel symbolizes:

> Transparency. What you are in private is what you are in public.
>
> Integrity. You are known for what is inside of you.
>
> A good name, more desirable than great wealth (see Proverbs 22:1)
>
> Grace to walk in a manner worthy of your calling (see Ephesians 4)

Read the following prayer aloud over yourself:

> Father, this is my prayer—that I would walk in a manner worthy of the calling with which I have been called, that by humility and gentleness, with patience and diligence, I would preserve the unity of the Spirit in the bond of peace (see Ephesians 4:1–3).
>
> I pray that Your gifts would be bestowed in Your time and wisdom upon me, a supernatural steward.
>
> I pray I would attain to the unity of the faith, and of the knowledge of the Son of God, to a mature person, to the measure of the stature that belongs to the fullness of Christ (see Ephesians 4:13).
>
> May I no longer be tossed here and there as a child. Rather, may I speak the truth in love and grow up in all aspects into Christ (see Ephesians 4:14–15).
>
> May I be united with the Body of Christ, my mind being renewed and my speech true and redeemed (see Ephesians 4:16–31).

Finally, may I continue tenderhearted as I serve You as a Prosperous Soul. I pray these things in Jesus' name. Amen.

Place your hand on your heart and declare, "I am a Prosperous Soul."

Beloved, I pray that in all respects you may prosper and be in good health, just as your soul prospers.

3 John 1:2

LESSONS
Chapter 7

HOMEWORK

Practice the Turning in the River exercise each day for one month. Write out the testimony of what God shows you while you're standing in the river. Pay close attention to the lessons learned facing downstream as well as facing upstream. Journal how you feel.

VIDEO

Watch "Dominion" on your DVD or in the online curriculum.

GOING DEEPER

How does facing God's throne position you for abundance? Have you found yourself facing downstream when God was calling you upstream?

What surprises or realizations came up as you were turning in the river?

Are there good and better things taking up room in your life? What boundaries can you set so that you can choose God's best?

How can turning in the river help you to align yourself with God's perspective?

What would it look like to have dominion over your calling and finances?

FURTHER STUDY

Read *Money and the Prosperous Soul* (chapter 8).

Read or memorize Revelation 22:1–2.

Explore the subjects of authority, the tree of life, and dominion in the Bible.

Review Tokens 9, 10, and 11 (river stone, cinnamon stick, and nickel).

PRAYER

Help me, Father, to walk in a manner worthy of Your calling. Help me to be patient and trusting as I position myself in the river for Your endless blessings. Thank You that You have all the days of my life planned out in advance. I am safe to remain in Your timing. Finally, help me, Lord, to remain tenderhearted—that I might serve You well as a Prosperous Soul. I pray this in Jesus' name. Amen.

PROPHETIC ACT

Declare this over your life: "I am in dominion, under heaven's authority, and a co-heir with Christ."

EXTRA RESOURSES

Book: Bridges, Jerry. *The Pursuit of Holiness*. Colorado Springs, CO: The Navigators, 1978.

Book: Hartley, Robert. *The Call to the Wall*. Overland Park, KS: New Grid Publishing, 2006.

Book: Wilkinson, Bruce. *The Prayer of Jabez*. Sisters, OR: Multnomah Publishers, Inc., 2000.

Chapter 8
AFTERTHOUGHTS

"I will prosper and be in good health,
even as my soul prospers."

FINAL SUGGESTIONS

Now that we have gone through this journey of the Prosperous Soul: Foundations manual, I have a few requests and suggestions:

Read Appendix B – Bethel Offering Declarations aloud. These are the declarations made over offerings by the congregation of Bethel Church of Redding, CA.

Create and read aloud your own declarations.

Continue praying aloud the following prayer:

I am facing upstream by the grace of God.
I can see the throne of God and the Lamb.

Good things are coming to me.
The good things are everywhere, here in the river.

There is more than I can contain.
There is abundance here for everyone.
Even for me. I receive Your good gifts in Jesus' name.

Amen.

We would love to hear your testimonies. You can submit them online. Just go to www.stephenkdesilva.com.

Ask God to provide you with your twelfth token. Pursue the Holy Spirit on what your token means prophetically, and write out the meaning and significance for yourself and your life.

TOKEN 12: ?

Prophetically, the final token symbolizes:

_____

_____

_____

Write down what you see and hear.

As a final wrap-up to the manual and class, take the Prosperous Soul Quiz and see where you rank after you have been working so hard to adopt the principles of a Prosperous Soul. Go to www.stephenkdesilva.com.

NEW PRACTICES

Take a moment and write down anything God may speak to you now about new practices He would like you to incorporate.

LESSONS
Chapter 8

HOMEWORK

Find your own token and work out what it prophetically symbolizes. If you wish, you can help us build a world-class product by sharing your testimonies and reviews at www.stephenkdesilva.com. You can also email your results to hello@stephenkdesilva.com.

VIDEO

Watch "Roots of Trust" on your DVD or in the online curriculum.

GOING DEEPER

How has this course affected your thinking on God, yourself, and money?

How has this curriculum helped you in becoming a Prosperous Soul?

What has been the most difficult and the most inspiring part of this curriculum?

What is one thing you will start doing as a result of this course?

What is one thing you will stop doing as a result of this course?

What is one thing you will change as a result of this course?

Is there someone you could share this manual with?

FURTHER STUDY

Read *Money and the Prosperous Soul* (chapter 9).

Read or memorize 3 John 1:2.

Review Token 12.

PRAYER

Thank You, Father, that I am a Prosperous Soul. I position myself for Your blessings and am excited to see what we will accomplish together. Keep my heart and my mind and my soul aligned with You. I pray this in Jesus' name. Amen.

PROPHETIC ACT

Declare this over your life: *"I will prosper and be in good health, even as my soul prospers."*

EXTRA RESOURSES

Book: Johnson, Bill. *Strengthen Yourself in the Lord.* Shippensburg, PA: Destiny Image Publishers, Inc., 2007.

Book: Seuss, Dr. *Oh, the Places You'll Go.* Random House, 1990.

Prosperous Soul | Foundations

TOKEN KEY

PENNY

Prophetically, the penny symbolizes:

First or beginning. This begins your journey of a prosperous soul.

Liberty is different from freedom because liberty implies the ability to choose between many possibilities and freedom implies release or escape from a threat. A prosperous soul will learn to grow beyond freedom into liberty (the capacity to choose well between many opportunities). Because prosperity and riches can make a way for good and evil, a prosperous soul must learn to restrain him/herself. The penny reminds us to mature in our capacity to carry liberty.

Abraham Lincoln said, "Any man can withstand adversity, if you wish to test a man's character, give him power."

The United States' motto: In God We Trust. This speaks of the need to trust in God, not money.

GLASS BEAD

Prophetically, the glass bead symbolizes:

Reawakening the dreamer in you (See Genesis 37:19).

The first rule of success: *If you can't dream it, you can't have it.*

Violent reaction against the scheme of the evil one (See Matthew 11:12).

ONE MILLION-DOLLAR BILL

Prophetically, the one million-dollar bill symbolizes:

The understanding that money is power, and power exaggerates whatever is in the heart.

A supernatural steward's willingness to deal with the issues of the heart.

The steward's access to receive or possess power in the form of money, riches, and wealth.

The great responsibility to manage wealth for Christ intentionally and wisely.

PAIR OF DIMES

Prophetically, the two dimes symbolize:

A paradigm (pair of dimes) shift from the poverty spirit to a prosperous soul (See Colossians 1:13).

Ten or tenth stands for our living sacrifice to God (See Romans 12:1).

Sanctification and purification (See Hebrews 10:10).

PAPERCLIP

Prophetically, the paper clip symbolizes:

The circular, possessive nature of the poverty spirit.

The poverty spirit's design to hold you.

Bents (bends) in our lives toward a beggarly attitude.

MUSTARD SEEDS

Prophetically, the seeds symbolize:

That ideas are seeds able to reproduce themselves.

Truth is formed when we believe ideas, whether those ideas are good or evil.

The creative power in us to create the environment around us from what is inside.

We act upon what we believe to be true.

RUBBER BAND

Prophetically, the rubber band symbolizes:

The flexible nature of being bound in spirit to something.

The necessity of being held to something bigger than yourself.

Courage to persevere in the face of enemy schemes.

ALUMINUM FOIL

Prophetically, the aluminum foil symbolizes:

The shiny appeal of Mammon.

The ability of Mammon to wrap around anything if we are not careful and aware.

The inherent usefulness of unrighteous Mammon.

RIVER STONE

Prophetically, the river stone symbolizes:

Your position in the crystal river of time (See Revelations 22).

Spiritual maturity to walk as an owner and co-heir of the kingdom.

Authority to demonstrate heaven's credentials (following signs).

Dominion as a prosperous soul.

CINNAMON STICK

Prophetically, the cinnamon symbolizes:

Anointing – an original element of anointing oil (See Exodus 30:22-2).

Preservation – historically used to preserve meat.

Nourishment – the only raw spice that is edible.

Intimacy – a perfumer's ingredient.

Healing – historically used as a medicine.

NICKEL

Prophetically, the nickel symbolizes:

Transparency – what you are in private is what you are in public.

Integrity – what is inside of you is what you are known for.

A good name, more desirable than great wealth (See Proverbs 22:1).

Grace to walk in a manner worthy of the calling (See Ephesians 4).

?

Prophetically, the_____symbolizes:

_____

_____

_____

APPENDIX A
The Voyage

The following excerpt is the introduction to Stephen's book, Money and the Prosperous Soul.[6]

We can find ourselves in a good book. Stories can spark perspective, hope, and victory in a person's life. My prayer for you is that the following pages would spark the journey of your own prosperous soul. To that end, imagine you are on a voyage.

You are the captain of a cargo ship, responsible to acquire, protect, manage and deliver merchandise for its rightful owners—you are a steward. In spite of your skills as a sailor, you have suffered loss from time to time. Foul weather has required you to jettison cargo, doldrums have threatened, but you have sailed on through tempests and calm. This is your profession; you are a dealer and transporter of goods from port to port.

Then one day you receive a great commission—a voyage that will require you to sail far beyond the familiar harbors and stretches of ocean. The risks are great, but the reward is greater. The one who has chartered your ship is the most successful merchant in the world. He is looking for business partners, and this voyage is to be the first stage leading to a permanent partnership. When he approaches, you are skeptical that your small-time cargo ship may not be a viable candidate for his fleet. But he quickly explains that your craft will be refitted at many of the ports on the journey in order to accommodate the accumulating goods. Your task is to deliver these goods at a final destination on a faraway shore. It is the opportunity of a lifetime, so you accept.

The next day you weigh anchor and set sail for open seas. You look out and see the jagged contours of the mountainous islands that have long stood tall and menacing at the borders of your usual trade routes. Concealed rocks and shallows around these islands have wrecked many a ship and often damaged your own. Strange currents have swept some vessels in eddying circles for months and years. But though these islands are notorious for their dangers, but you and your crew have sailed here for generations. You've become comfortable in these familiar waters.

You study a map provided by the merchant. It reveals a different perspective on the dangerous chain of islands; they are marked with a simple word: *Poverty*. The map reveals that these islands obstruct your course. You must first navigate past them and leave them behind for unknown waters. Thus, your first new challenge is simply to abandon routine, which isn't easy. As dangerous as these islands have been, at least they were *familiar*. You felt confident sailing around them, even when they threatened destruction.

Gradually, your courage rises and you sail on, stretching the distance between your ship and those perilous shores. The mountains melt in your wake, leaving you alone in a vast ocean with only a strange map and one dim hope.

---

6   Stephen K. De Silva, Money and the Prosperous Soul: Tipping the Scales of Favor and Blessing (Ada, MI: Chosen Books, 2010.)

Far ahead a new land appears. Pulling out the map, you notice there are more details than before—the map is expanding as your voyage progresses. Not only do you see a new string of islands, but the map reveals their name: *Mammon*. You realize that although these two island chains are beyond each other's sight, they fashion a corridor between which you must navigate. The map becomes vital, stressing unconventional course settings and highlighting menacing threats. Negotiating every new hazard, each distinct but all potentially disastrous to your voyage, constantly requires you to abandon your old trusted methods and learn new ones.

You continue to fix your course upon the merchant's destination, learning to trust the map, which always brings you safely to each port along the way. Just as the merchant had promised, there are outfitters at every port to restore and refit your ship, expanding its capacity and strength. Gradually, off in the distance, a faint shape forms on the horizon. Looking to the map, you catch your breath. A new country has emerged on the page. It is a vast continent, deep with promise, which the map simply names: *Destiny*.

Poverty and Mammon are spiritual influences that we all must learn to resist. Each of these spirits, like the islands in the voyage, has its own current, pulling upon our internal wounds and fears like magnets, and each features a host of pitfalls, both literal and spiritual, that are disastrous to wealth. Some believers perceive these influences as normal or unavoidable parts of everyday life—let's call them *familiar spirits*—and unintentionally allow their destructive effects into their lives. Other believers overcompensate in their avoidance of one spirit, putting themselves at risk of falling under the power of the other. We must continually consult the Holy Spirit for guidance and allow Him to train our vision upon our ultimate goal—Jesus, the one who has gone before us as our model of stewardship and the embodiment of the prosperous soul.

Where, you might ask, does a prosperous soul feature in this voyage story? It is the ship itself, where the condition of our souls is like the capacity of a ship. It determines what we can be entrusted to carry. Just as the islands threaten the ship, the dangers of Poverty and Mammon are targeted primarily at diminishing our soul's capacity, not merely our material possessions and circumstances. But the One who calls us to this journey does the opposite, growing our ability to carry wealth, both natural and spiritual. Our cooperation with God causes our souls to expand, according to John's prayer, even as our *soul prospers* (3 John 1:2).

APPENDIX B
Offering Readings

OFFERING OF THANKS #1

As we receive today's offering, we are believing the Lord for:

Jobs and better jobs, raises and bonuses, benefits, sales and commissions, favorable settlements, estates and inheritances, interests and income, rebates and returns, checks in the mail, gifts and surprises, finding money, debts paid off, expenses decrease, blessing and increase.

Thank You, Lord, for meeting all of my financial needs—that I may have more than enough to give into the kingdom of God and promote the gospel of Jesus Christ. Hallelujah!

OFFERING OF THANKS #2

As we receive today's offering, we are believing You for:

Heaven opened, earth invaded, storehouses unlocked, and miracles created, dreams and visions, angelic visitations, declarations, and divine manifestations. Anointings, giftings, and calls, positions and promotions, provisions and resources to go to the nations. Souls and more souls from every generation, saved and set free, carrying kingdom revelation.

Thank You, Father, that as I join my value system to Yours, You will shower favor, blessings, and increase upon me so I have more than enough to co-labor with heaven and see Jesus get His full reward. Hallelujah!

OFFERING OF THANKS #3

As we pray for new wells of revival, we pray for new economic wells in Redding to be created. So, Lord, we ask You for:

Favor for our city with CEOs, government leaders, and kings. Manufacturing firms that produce goods for the nations and provide new jobs for our people. Technology to establish new markets, energy sources, and efficient solutions to grow as a population. Laws and courts that measure with the justice and the freedom of our land's constitution. Civil servants that encourage entrepreneurs. Media known for wisdom and truth. Natural resources released, harvested, sold, and reproduced. Education, books, and universities that develop mind molders who influence the influential. Capital to build small businesses that provide services. Arts and culture attracting both young and old. Medical community known for integrity and excellence. Repentance from poverty, small thinking, and envy. Courage to recognize opportunities and make wealth. Abundance to bless the world and the prudence to save and invest. Revelation to pass on wealth to our children's children.

So we declare that when the righteous prosper, the city rejoices!

APPENDIX C
Curious List of Lies

EXPOSING LIES WE BELIEVE IN EXCHANGE FOR ETERNAL TRUTH

The following is a condensed list of actual phrases identified by former *Prosperous Soul* students. It is provided here as a tool to help you identify your own lies held in your heart, which destructively affect your life. These lies must be exposed and exchanged for biblical truth; therefore, each lie is *followed by the antithetical truth in italics.* The list cannot be exhaustive because of the personal nature of how we individually process past events and circumstances of life.

I began to survey students' responses to chapter 4, "Root of Truth," as a teaching tool to help them identify lies they believed deeply enough to affect their lives. I've found that many of us hold lies as truth, and usually these lies are associated with father wounds of provision and identity.

I encourage you to confront the unhealthy core beliefs in your life and seek a Bethel Sozo or other counseling in order to end destructive behaviors and build toward a Prosperous Soul (see 3 John 1:2). Seek truth from the Bible, and plant this truth deeply in your heart. Learn to live from the truth that God is for you and He is in a good mood.

LIES BASED IN FEAR - EXPECTATION OF PUNISHMENT

…But Perfect Love Casts Out Fear (see 1 John 4:18)

Money scares me. I live in constant fear about money.
- *Fretting is not my portion (see Psalm 37 and Proverbs 24:19).*

Something has to go wrong because I'm feeling way too good.
- *Dread is the possession of evildoers and not the Christian (see Jeremiah 20:11).*

I'll lose all of my possessions. I'll be left with nothing.
- *I am a city not forsaken (see Isaiah 62:12).*

My past mistakes must ruin my future.
- *I have a future, and my hope is never cut off (see Proverbs 23:18).*

I'm afraid God won't prosper me.
- *Prosperity is my portion and promise (see Deuteronomy 8:18).*

I am not enough. I'm insignificant.
- *I can do all things in Christ (see Ephesians 1:10).*

I'm afraid of failing when God doesn't show up.
- *God hasn't given me a spirit of fear (see 2 Timothy 1:7).*

God won't bless me because I may self-destruct.
- *My character is free from the love of money (see Hebrews 13:5).*

It's too late and I'm too old to get wealthy.
- *God's promises apply to me regardless of my age (see Genesis 17:17).*

LIES BASED IN VALUE – MISSING OR DISTORTED IDENTITY

…Yet Christ Has Accepted Us to the Glory of God (see Romans 15:7)

What I think doesn't matter.
- *My ideas matter because I have the mind of Christ (see 1 Corinthians 2:16).*

I always feel rejected by people, by God, by myself.
- *The cross qualifies me to draw near with confidence (see Hebrews 4:16).*

My value depends on my intelligence, strength, or physical beauty.
- *God gave us value, and it is by grace alone, not works (see Ephesians 2:8).*

I am less than others. There's something wrong with me because I don't fit in.
- *I am precious to God and one of His children (see Titus 2:11).*

I am a failure because of past failures.
- *God's mercies are new every morning (see Lamentations 3:22–25).*

I don't deserve love, money, or health. I'll always be the poor one in the family.
- *If I am humble and fear God, the reward is riches, honor, and life (see Proverbs 22:4).*

I am worthless and not good enough for success.
- *Christ loves me and died on the cross for me (see John 3:16).*

I don't deserve to be wealthy because I haven't been good enough with money.
- *I can be faithful in small things and leave the rest to God (see Luke 16:10).*

I shouldn't ask for things. Whenever I do, I am ignored or put in my place.
- *We can ask God in confidence, knowing He hears us (see 1 John 5:14).*

I am a pauper, not a prince or princess.
- *Christ's sacrifice delivered me from darkness into light (see Colossians 1:13).*

I am a burden to my family and society.
- *I received supernatural power to become a world changer (see Acts 1:8).*

I am not loved. I'm adopted because no one wanted me.
- *I am dearly loved and adopted as a son or daughter into Jesus Christ Himself (see Ephesians 1:5).*

God is too big and too busy to pay attention to me.
- *God's eye is upon me. I am not forgotten (see Luke 12:24).*

LIES BASED ON EXTERNAL FORCES – VICTIM SPIRIT, EXPLOITATION

…But No Weapon Formed Against Me Shall Prosper (see Isaiah 54:17)

My family is cursed. I am cursed and can't break free.
- *Every curse without cause does not alight (see Proverbs 26:2).*

Life is always a struggle; circumstances and problems rule my life.
- *God is my refuge and my strength (see Psalm 46:1).*

I will fail because of my enemies. I am destined to be poor.
- *I can rest in the Lord and see His deliverance (see Psalm 37:7–11).*

I am jobless and can't work.
- *God will supply all your needs (see Philippians 4:19).*

I feel attacked and vulnerable.
- 	*God is a strong tower where I can hide (see Proverbs 18:10).*

Because of my age, I am overlooked. I'm powerless.
- 	*God has given you the power to make wealth (see Deuteronomy 8:18).*

LIES BASED IN HOPELESSNESS – BEARING UNDER A BROKEN SPIRIT

…Our Sure and Steadfast Hope Is an Anchor of the Soul (see Hebrews 6:19)

God will not ever come to my home.
- 	*I am not hidden from God, even in times of trouble (see Psalm 33:18).*

I can't know my purpose in life.
- 	*I am God's poem, created for good works in Christ (see Ephesians 2:10).*

I am incapable of stewardship. I can't get control of myself or my money.
- 	*I can do all things in Christ (see Philippians 4:13).*

I will never get the things I really want. I'll never thrive or have financial peace.
- 	*Desire fulfilled is a tree of life (see Proverbs 13:12).*

I always end up alone. I'm so lonely.
- 	*I am a member of the family of Christ (see 1 John 1:7).*

I always end up codependent.
- 	*I am powerful and able to wage war against hopelessness (see Matthew 11:12).*

I have lost everything, including hope.
- 	*I am powerful and able to wage war against hopelessness (see Matthew 11:12).*

Things and problems in my life will never change forever.
- 	*Times will change, and there are appointed times for everything (see Ecclesiastes 3:1).*

Life will always be a struggle and I'll never get ahead.
- 	*Rest and peace are my portion through Christ (see Hebrews 4:9–11).*

I have no one to leave an inheritance to, so why bother?
- *I am adding to a great inheritance as one of God's saints (see Ephesians 3:21).*

God will not provide for my wants, only my needs.
- *Desire fulfilled is a tree of life (see Proverbs 13:12).*

LIES ABOUT MONEY – DESTRUCTIVE PATTERNS AND JEOPARDY

…Yet Our Great Wealth Is in the House of the Righteous (see Proverbs 15:6)

The rich are unhappy.
- *I rejoice at the bountiful fruit of my hands (see Psalm 128:2).*

You have to have money to get money.
- *It is my God who gives me seed to sow (see 2 Corinthians 9:10).*

Money diverts you from the kingdom.
- *Money is a tool, and true wealth is Christ Himself (see Colossians 2:2).*

I feel guilty about having money because money is evil.
- *Wealth is a tool in my hand. I am free of the love of money (see 1 Timothy 6:10).*

I have to have money to make money.
- *God has given me the power to make wealth (see Deuteronomy 8:18).*

I'll never be able to get out of debt. I feel trapped.
- *I am a firmly planted tree, and I will prosper (see Psalm 1:3).*

If I own my own business, I will not prosper or succeed.
- *I will see my appointed harvest. God brings rain to dry lands (see Jeremiah 5:24).*

Money is a distraction. It controls you.
- *I am content, and my love belongs to Christ alone (see Hebrews 13:5).*

You can't follow the Lord and have money, too.
- *I am a servant of Christ and a steward of His mysteries (see 1 Corinthians 4:1).*

FURTHER RESOURCES

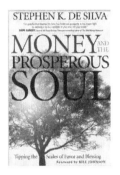

Money and the Prosperous Soul / Book

When it comes to money, why does it seem as if we're always one step behind? Stephen says the answer is not just about how you handle what's in your bank account, but it's also spiritual. In a warm, conversational style, he combines practical financial teaching with sound biblical truth. Discover the supernatural keys to breaking free from destructive financial cycles. Don't wait—start living a truly prosperous life right now.

Prosperous Soul Master Course, Volume 1 / Manual

Volume One in the four-volume series entitled Prosperous Soul Master Course examines the philosophical and doctrinal moorings of biblical stewardship. It establishes a sound mode of thinking about the purpose behind self, money, and supernatural stewardship.

Prosperous Soul Master Course, Volume 2 / Manual

Volume Two in the four-volume series entitled Prosperous Soul Master Course examines the practical and spiritual mechanisms of money, along with biblically based tools, prayers, and prophetic exercises designed for identifying and overcoming faulty mechanisms.

Prosperous Soul Master Course, Volume 3 / Manual

Volume Three explores scriptural ways of stewarding riches and offers more advanced tools for affecting your financial environment, such as generosity, rest, resilience, and inquiry.

Prosperous Soul Master Course, Volume 4 / Manual

Volume Four explores the similarities and differences between sacred and secular elements of supernatural stewardship. Learn from gifted stewards gone before us, financial champions who are examined like case studies for truths and secrets, as well as pitfalls to be avoided.

Prosperous Home, Volume 1 / Manual

Do you constantly feel out of control with your finances? Are you looking to make changes that catapult you into a thriving life? Stephen's unique perspective on how to manage money well comes from a belief that money is a spiritual power. The solution to managing money well is not just to try harder but to understand how we approach money. In this manual you will learn how to budget well, how to think about debt, and how to spend with purpose.

Financial Sozo / Manual

Financial Sozo is a tool designed for leaders and Sozo ministers who want to delve deeper into the important area of financial deliverance. Building on the work of the Sozo ministry, Stephen De Silva explains what is going on "behind the scenes" in his popular classes Prosperous Soul Foundations Course and Prosperous Soul Master Course. Learn about Stephen's four-step process, what a Financial Sozo is, discover the three spheres of poverty, and access the secrets of today's Kingdom economy. This teaching sheds new light on the old problem of overcoming crippling financial patterns in the lives of those God sets before us.

ABOUT
Stephen K. De Silva Ministries

Much is taught about the subject of stewardship but seldom is the purpose and nature of money explained. Stephen K. De Silva Ministries is changing the conversation about money. Money is a servant with the power to exaggerate the heart of its master. This power will manifest in both economic and spiritual ways, and this dualism has been ignored to our own peril. Until now.

Stephen is expanding the story of wealth, riches, and how to master money using biblical truth. Financial problems are rarely about money. Learn how to exit the bitter struggle between poverty and mammon by severing the source of every financial disease: the orphan spirit. Overcome generational cycles of loss and harm, and advance yourself for good. Join us on this journey and become the steward God imagined you to be; become a Prosperous Soul.

DIVISIONS OF STEPHEN K. DE SILVA MINISTRIES

Stephen K. De Silva Ministries currently operates in six different areas. You can access material and training in these areas through our physical, digital, and online resources; by going to our classes or conferences; or by receiving coaching or a Financial Sozo from our team. Find out more at www.stephenkdesilva.com.

PROSPEROUS SOUL	Prosperous Soul is the flagship ministry focused on the heart and soul. This ministry deals with the root causes of why we do what we do and catapults us into true biblical stewardship.
PROSPEROUS HOME	Prosperous Home brings the practical finance tools to your home while building on a unique perspective: dealing with the motivation behind your decisions. This ministry is designed to elevate your understanding of money in your life and show you how to master it to accomplish your God-given purpose.
PROSPEROUS ENTERPRISE	Prosperous Enterprise takes entrepreneurs and small businesses to the next level. This ministry brings wisdom and tools to your business to accelerate your growth and refine your purpose, so you can streamline your vision and create a prosperous enterprise.
PROSPEROUS CHURCH	This ministry is focused on bringing biblical finance structure in your church or ministry. Through leadership coaching and biblical teaching, learn how to marry biblical stewardship with supernatural faith.
PURPOSE TRAIN	This unique ministry is designed to bring breakthrough in your decisions and give executive coaching, so you can operate fully from who you are and who you are meant to be.
FINANCIAL SOZO	Financial Sozo is a counseling and coaching ministry designed to bring breakthrough and financial deliverance. You can receive Financial Sozos and learn how to be a part of Stephen's team facilitating Financial Sozos.

ABOUT
The Author

STEPHEN K. DE SILVA began his professional career in 1985 as a certified public accountant. From 1995 until 2017, he ran an exclusive service company specializing in nonprofit accounting and ministerial income tax preparation while simultaneously leading a growing team as Chief Financial Officer and member of the Senior Leadership Team for Bethel Church of Redding. Stephen's unique blend of experience, training, and integrity makes him a pioneer expert at the subject of money. Now as a full-time international speaker, author, and thought leader, Stephen releases purpose, excellence, and generosity in place of financial fear, confusion, and greed.